THE ANGELS WON'T HELP YOU

Before you start to read this book, take this moment to think about making a donation to punctum books, an independent non-profit press,

@ https://punctumbooks.com/support/

If you're reading the e-book, you can click on the image below to go directly to our donations site. Any amount, no matter the size, is appreciated and will help us to keep our ship of fools afloat. Contributions from dedicated readers will also help us to keep our commons open and to cultivate new work that can't find a welcoming port elsewhere. Our adventure is not possible without your support.

Vive la Open Access.

Fig. 1. Detail from Hieronymus Bosch, *Ship of Fools* (1490–1500)

First published in 2022 by dead letter office, BABEL Working Group, an imprint of punctum books, Earth, Milky Way.
https://punctumbooks.com

The BABEL Working Group is a collective and desiring-assemblage of scholar–gypsies with no leaders or followers, no top and no bottom, and only a middle. BABEL roams and stalks the ruins of the post-historical university as a multiplicity, a pack, looking for other roaming packs with which to cohabit and build temporary shelters for intellectual vagabonds. BABEL is an experiment in ephemerality. Find us if you can.

ISBN-13: 978-1-68571-050-7 (print)
ISBN-13: 978-1-68571-051-4 (ePDF)

DOI: 10.53288/0388.1.00

LCCN: 2022951504
Library of Congress Cataloging Data is available from the Library of Congress

Book design: Vincent W.J. van Gerven Oei

p. punctumbooks
DLO
spontaneous acts of scholarly combustion

HIC SVNT MONSTRA

M.H.
Bowker

The Angels Won't
Help You

p.

Contents

Acknowledgments

I am profoundly indebted to Eileen A. Fradenburg Joy for years of inspiration, generosity, and support. This project, like many others, would have been inconceivable without her help.

I am equally grateful to Vincent W.J. van Gerven Oei, whose immensely thoughtful work has made this and other punctum books into realities.

Early versions of portions of the essay, "*Hikikomori, Amae,* and Help," were published in *The Journal of Psychosocial Studies* 9, no. 1 (2016): 20–52.

For Julie, who knows how to help

To the Reader

O please help. This is not a cry for help. This is not a call to arms. I am not kneeling down or with cupped hands pleading piously. This is a contemplation. No one understands.

People talk of "care," don't see why anybody should be concerned with "help." Some friends were discussing the Olympics, saying they liked the backstories the TV ran and ran. I said these bored me and my friends replied, "But they make you care about the athletes."

Why should I care about the athletes? Would I appreciate their performances more? Would I suffer their victories and losses with them?[1] It is not cold-hearted to say that I do not care about these people. Likewise, if I am saddened by tragedies near or far, I cannot say, wish as I might, that I care about their victims. For the most part, I do not know them. How could I care about them?

Wallace Stevens called the "pressure of reality" the extraordinary nature of news, world and national events, and the direst circumstances affecting our lives: wars, pandemics, recessions,

---

1   Yes, in theory. The point of human-interest stories, in this context, is to feed viewers enough emotional content that they identify with the athletes, so they keep watching the TV, even during truck commercials, with which they also identify.

resurgences of fascism, and so on. Such events exert an extraordinary "pressure […] on the consciousness to the exclusion of any power of contemplation" (1951, 20). The problem with extraordinary pressures on the consciousness is that they degrade the imagination as it [the imagination] loses touch with reality, cannot comprehend or make use of it, and, thus, comes to lack vitality. Not only is our imagination denigrated — an outcome horrific enough in itself — but our ability to respond to the crises of today with thoughtful, imaginative solutions is likewise jeopardized.

> Rightly or wrongly, we feel that the fate of a society is involved in the orderly disorders of the present time. We are confronting, then, a set of events, not only beyond our power to tranquilize them in the mind, beyond our power to reduce and metamorphose them, but events that stir the emotions to violence, that engage us in what is direct and immediate and real, and events that involve the concepts and sanctions that are the order of our lives and may involve our very lives; and these events are occurring persistently with increasing omen, in what may be called our presence. (Stevens 1951, 22)

Faced with such a situation — and is it possible to read the above and not to recognize a depiction of our present predicament? — and given that "our presence" now extends globally, exchanging information from across the world at an incredible velocity, we may well feel called to care, to help, or both. What are we to do?

While care is easier to imagine, care may lose contact with the realities of the cared-for. The widely held belief that "those who help care" or that "people help because they care" does not hold up to scientific scrutiny (Nadler 2000, 76–80). Likewise, the notion that we can solve the world's problems by caring is a fantasy. In some cases, people claim to care about others with whom and with whose predicaments they are wholly unfamiliar. Even contemplating the disasters with which we are so frequently confronted may be too difficult, for contemplation happens when both reality and the imagination are engaged and balanced.

Let us say that, pressured as we are, we imaginatively unimaginatively turn to care — what Freud would recognize as a diffuse love for humankind — and turn away from help, because help confronts us with a new reality of ourselves and others, opens up the possibility of creating something new, indeed, requires the establishment of a new, real relationship between helper and helpee. Those without histories of well-functioning helping relationships (where help was not exploitative, destructive, or traumatic) will have a hard time imagining how to establish one (either as helper or helpee) in adult life. In addition to such individual and familiar factors, the greater the pressure of reality on such individuals, the more likely they are to repress (re-press) that which they could not survive as children (i.e., the exploitation, destruction, or trauma), hiding it away from contemplation into unconsciousness.

To press. Pressure is repressive. I once had a mother. Too much pressure and repression. Pressure cooking. Pressure even cooking. Cooking is a metaphor for not being cooked for.

Here is a paradox. Reality and the imagination are interdependent. Help, I wish to argue, is more psychologically and politically valuable than care — which is not to say that emotions are less important than actions nor that emotions ought to be assessed according to their psychological and political "value" or use, which, itself, would evince a surrender to the pressure of reality — but, at the same time, help cannot be taken lightly because help involves real relationships initiated and negotiated between persons.

Help involves relating and acting rather than merely adopting what might be described as a caring mental attitude. Amidst an increasing pressure of reality, it is not uncommon to find individuals seeking solutions to the world's real problems by attempting to fix in the imagination — as if changing our Facebook profile picture would change the world — what is broken in reality (see Bowker 2014). But, at the same time, the imagination falters as it loses (or gives up) contact with the reality of the other needed to create a relationship of help. Help, like true empathy, is based on a balance of imagination and reality: One must overcome the pressure of reality to find, as it were, enough ground on which to base the imaginary–real relationship of help.

§

Let me begin again. Help is the fundamental and active element of care. In the case of help, we do not experience the other as an extension of the self, with whom we can identify. Help is given and received in the space between self and other. Care lives inside self and other and, in some cases, collapses the space between self and other to create a unity — that is altogether different from help — through sympathy or love.

It is possible to care without helping. It is also possible to help without caring. Given these two options, most people would choose the second, especially in difficult moments.[2]

Dear reader, this is an honest book.[3] I have sought help in writing it mainly but not solely via others' published works. Perhaps this is because I found myself quite anxious that receiving even a modicum of "living," real-time ("real"–"time") help from

---

2   I still imagine that I care about the global poor but went to West Africa thinking my care would help. It did not. My caring was my need for help in solidifying an identity as someone who cares. Who cares and suffers. And the suffering persons I imagined to care for helped me. This happens all the time.

3   That is a line I have stolen from Michel de Montaigne (1533–92) with whom I have no wish to compare myself.

a friend or colleague would steal the book, make it foreign, and leave it, in the end, incomprehensible to me.[4]

If the mad learned psychology who would know. No one would know they knew. No one would know they were mad. No one would know what they learned.

I have tried to resist this anxiety in order to make use of such help. To the extent that I have succeeded, I did so by separating help from care; that is, separating the fact that I care about my friend or colleague from the fact that the friend or colleague had little to offer or offered unhelpful advice. Once separated, I could reject help without rejecting a friend.

Several colleagues with whom I spoke expressed an interest in obligations put upon *recipients* of help. While this is undoubtedly an important problem, one addressed in what follows, the concern also reflects inner conflicts about help and hurt, which may include both the unconscious hatred of help and the desire to hurt those who need help.

We say: "Maybe we are helping too much; maybe we are not helping enough; maybe the helpee is feeling impinged upon; maybe our help is taking something important away from the helpee, like dignity or autonomy; maybe our help has made us a central figure in someone's (or some group's) emotional life, maybe helping is draining us of our lives," and so on.

If help takes "something important away" from the recipient, we may well ask how this process and this "something" are related to helpers' (presumptive) *wish* to take away pain, sorrow, or distress from helpees. In psychological terms, perhaps our *wish* — to unburden and take away pain, sorrow, or distress from the helpee — is ambivalent and charged with anxiety; after all, we do not want to become so burdened and taxed that

---

4   Such anxiety of influence is considerably neurotic, paranoid, likely related to a host of horrifying psychological problems, including rage against help: a defense organized around failures of help so grave that they could only be internalized as vicious attacks on the self.

we must then ask for help for ourselves. At the same time, the more we confuse help with care, the more we long for closeness with those cared-for, confusing closeness with an active aspect of care (i.e., help). We hope that, via an identification with the helpee, we will experience oneness with them (Maner et al. 2002), even if they are in great pain, and that this oneness is what they (or we) need.

Help and care are defining features of happy home environments but are not defining features of civil society.[5] Thus, diminishments of help, as changing conditions in the family nudge the growing child toward in-dependence, act as stark reminders of the difference between the home and the world outside. Twin ambivalent attractions, laden with unconscious personal and emotional meanings, obtain: seeking helpful contexts and environments (returning home) and refusing helpful contexts and environments (leaving home).

Of course, these impulses and their meanings can become confused if, for instance, one seeks to return "home" to an unhelpful context or system of meaning, or if a group becomes a traveling "home," organized around making its members or others helpless (Bowker and Levine 2018). It is a testament to the unconsciousness of our ambivalent desires for/against help that we debate about whether and how much help or care should make up the *normative* framework of civil society, i.e., moral theories about civil society (see de Sousa 2021).

Among others, Milton Mayeroff insists that "devotion is essential to caring" and that "obligations that derive from devotion are a constituent element in caring" (1971, 9). The danger here is expressed naively: "There is a convergence between what

---

5   By "civil society" I mean something like *koinōnia politikē* (κοινωνία πολιτική), the community in which we partake as citizens. There is, of course, a broader definition of civil society in which we could find examples of institutionalized help and care (healthcare or eldercare, for instance), but, as theorists of care would be quick to point out, we inhabit a society in which individuality and subjecthood are understood in terms of the attainment of independence and autonomy and not as interdependent members of groups.

I feel I am supposed to do and what I want to do" (9), a convergence owed to the increasingly enmeshed relationship between caregiver and recipient of care. If we are good caregivers, we feel devoted and obliged to care but must also follow the direction of the cared-for, despite the fact that "other-directed [care...] refers to the kind of conformity in which I lose touch with both myself and the other" (8).

The price for this conformity is *ressentiment,* a term that takes on its depth of meaning from Friedrich Nietzsche. *Ressentiment* means both a re-experiencing — "the repeated experiencing and reliving of a particular emotional response reaction against someone else" (Scheler 1961, 39) — and an emotional world full of envy and hostility, particularly with reference to those whose care takes from us something vital to ourselves. I submit that this vital thing is our imagination, as the experience of the cared-for takes up more and more room, as it were, in the inner world of the caregiver. Such envy and hostility may be expressed in the wish/worry that the cared-for have unpaid obligations to caregivers. These unpaid obligations become debts which, of course, privilege the creditor.

Aristotle, who seemed not to fully recognize the strangeness of his treatment of megalopsychia (magnanimity), claimed that it was a "crowning ornament of virtues" consisting of "conferring benefits but being ashamed to receive them as well as to try to outdo one's benefactor in return in order to retain a position of superiority" (Griffin 2013, 18).[6] If care leaves the helpee obliged to reciprocate but in a position where reciprocation is impossible, then we may have to go so far as to erase our care, so as not to encumber the recipient, as Jacques Derrida claims. Any gift "must not [be] perceived as a gift" (1992, 16) to avoid this dilemma. But Derrida is wrong. To be able to give and receive, to give thanks and to welcome thanks, are marks of maturity. In economic terms, whether the cost of care can be borne by both caregiver and cared-for is the question of care's relative value.

---

6   It is really in this sense that it is worth reading Marcel Mauss and Georges Bataille.

The relative value of help is greater than that of care on these terms.

§

O please understand. There are real caregivers and real helpers. They are not forcibly the same but they can be. Helpers help others, like children, the ailing, and the elderly, all the time, despite the costs, and despite egoistic theories of human motivation. So far, social psychology has not established a grounding for this behavior, other than to suggest that the drivers of helping are both a desire for "oneness" and an orthogonal drive to improve one's standing in "hierarchical" and competitive social and political relations (Nadler 2020).

In this book, I argue that while we may or may not find care in the home or in the world outside, what most of us need is help, that help is less likely to establish a hierarchical relation between helper and helpee, and that the costs of help are borne best in moments when both parties are focused on the "facilitative" function of helping: help that seeks to enable others to develop into themselves without, as in care, being so bound up with others and their well-being that helpee and helper become one.

What follows are essays of varying lengths, styles, and degrees of specificity, exploring the vicissitudes of help: its need, its failure, its value, its targets (who needs help), what happens when we find ourselves or others to be helpless, and more. I concentrate on failures of help and their consequences as much as I wish to focus on successful help, where two or more persons are brought momentarily "together" in a transitional space where facilitative interpretive contexts and systems of meaning allow helpees to strengthen themselves.

Help

I want to explore the concept of help, one that is pivotal to the practices of parenting and the rearing of children. Help is a non-clinical term, or, at least, is not typically restricted to clinical usage. Neither is help a "hot concept," as it is ignored by most psychosocial literatures as a subject of serious investigation.[1] This negligence is owed in part to help's near-synonymity with overlapping and widely discussed constructs, such as care and *caritas*.

Care and *caritas* are moral and sometimes spiritual-ethical ideals. Help is something less. Help possesses a far less ecclesiastical (surely less Augustinian or Thomistic) connotation than caritas, just as parents help children in countless ways, both caring and uncaring, magnificent and banal, instrumental and fa-

---

1   Help is ignored in part because the "standard narrative of contemporary psychoanalysis" (O'Loughlin 2001, 51) — if there be one — has come to include much of attachment theory, which is quite closely aligned with help. Indeed, it is a truism of the evolutionary, developmental, and psychosocial sciences that human beings are creatures for whom help is central to development (see Ainsworth et al. 1978; Bowlby 1969). Attachment theory has convincingly demonstrated that our emotional and intellectual lives are shaped, to a great degree, by the quality of our relationships with our parents and caregivers, relationships defined by children's profound reliance on others in early life.

cilitating (self-strengthening), all of whose moralities would be impossible to calculate.

To calculate moralities of care, to care and calculate moralities of care, is a sign of defeat. In defeat we calculate. Defeat that is predacious.

Caritas is too closely intertwined with love to help us contemplate help. You don't have to love someone to help them. You don't even have to care about them. Help doesn't have to be a virtue. Help is neither a spiritual nor intersubjective ideal.

For Augustine, *caritas* and *cupiditas* come from the same desire. There is no difference. *All* desire is craving (*appetitus*), even the rarified *caritas*. All love is acquisitive love ("Amor apepetitus quidam est"). This may also be called bonding: "The special role of *caritas,* expressed as bonding, understands the Divine in Man and Man in the Divine" (Day 2012, 13). *Caritas* is an appetite but for a different object, which is first and foremost divine. In *The City of God,* it is presented so simply as to imagine that cupiditas belongs to the city of man whereas *caritas* belongs to the city of God. There are at first but two possibilities, up or down: "Omnis amor aut ascendit aut descendit" [All love either ascends or descends] (Nygren 1953, 483). "In *caritas,* whose object is eternity, man transforms himself into an eternal, nonperishable being" (Arendt 1996, 18).

If there are three main Greek forms of love (*philia, eros,* and *agapē*), caritas derives from *agapē,* but "*agapē* […] is the love of the commandment. And it is an attitude, a will-disposition, a matter of the conative, not the emotive […] the result is that we are to love the unlikable. Only in this way can we make sure we grasp the meaning of 'Love your enemies'" (Fletcher 1967, 49).

The central argument for care ethics, in its origins (e.g., Gilligan 1982), was *not* based on *caritas* and was more squarely rooted in a rejection of the sovereign subject and of Enlightenment constructs of individual moral development and the rights and duties issuing from rational, male-oriented, occidental, Kantian ideals. But there has always been some link between the two constructs. *Caritas* is often represented as a woman with a child or children in her arms. And it was Adam Smith's treatment of beneficence that, well-before "care-ethics" became what it is today, that "afford[ed] a bridge between what might be called the virtues of *caritas* and the virtues of care" (Hanley 2009, 175–76).

What is more, to care *for* someone, we likely care *about* them in some way. The very word "care" invites us to consider the link between the desire of the caregiver and the needs of the cared-for, which may be fine for political theory but is not so good if you are thinking about situations where a person needs help. Here, a helpful parenting context, for instance, is one in which the needs of the child reliably outweigh the desires of the parent.

In the ideal parent–child relationship, the parent does not give help to bind to the child to the parent but to facilitate the development of what the child could be. The parent's desire should be, like the psychoanalyst's — neutral, the desire for "absolute difference" — which is to say that the parent should wish not that children become specific or given things, but only that children become themselves.

The most reliable indicator, then, of whether a person will give or receive help is not the presence of love or selflessness but the question of whether the person has internalized a benign and helpful internal world in which others may be helpers or recipients of help, depending on the context and the case. This is closer to Held's reasoning (1993).

It takes a bringing-heaven-down-to-Earth to make *caritas* the foundation of anything truly interpersonal, which is exactly what heaps of theorists, including Arendt to some degree (1996, 105–10), have done. They tie the love of God to the love of humankind or the community of fellows. Listen to John Angell James (1829), in his *Christian Charity Explained,* offer the following "example":

> How often have we beheld the dying Christian, who, during long and mortal sickness, has exhibited [...] something of the spirit of a glorified immortal [...]. The beams of heaven now falling upon his spirit were reflected [...] in the love which is the greatest in the trinity of Christian virtues. How lowly in his heart did he seem — how entirely clothed with humility! Instead of being puffed up with anything of his own [...] it was like a wound in his heart to hear anyone remind him either of his good deeds or dispositions [...]. Instead of envying the possessions or excellences of other men, it was a cordial to his departing spirit that he was leaving them thus distinguished: how kind was he to his friends!

I wonder if those who have cared for the elderly, the ill, for children, or for the dying would recognize in this sort of self-diminishment of their helpee an act of Christian virtue.

§

Even if secular, most specialists have argued that higher-order personal and social needs underlie the desire to help. Of these, the desires for belongingness and solidarity seem to get the majority of attention. Indeed, the "fundamental need" addressed by helping is the need for "belongingness that binds individuals and groups together" (Nadler 2020, 3).

Strange is that the primary negative outcome associated with help is damage to the recipient's sense of autonomy in the face of help's creation: a social hierarchy where the helpee is subordinated to the helper. Why not imagine that the development of just this hierarchy is what is aimed at (unconsciously) in helping that is associated with ideals like love and Christian charity? The more help provided, the more the helper is superior to the helpee. The helper is closer to God.

How far we have come from the Beatitudes. How far. How come.

Like care and *caritas,* help risks occluding the subjectivity of the helper and, ultimately, of the helpee, but, to prevent this, focusing on help permits us to ask critical questions about the former, e.g., whether love of humanity or divinity is really necessary for helping,[2] and, about the latter, whether the helpee will tolerate and benefit from help, based on contextual, historical, and psychological factors (see e.g., Coles 1997; Fisher, Nadler, and DePaulo 1983).

Help neatly and accurately defines its own work without the excessive burden of transforming this work into a universal moral, ethical, or spiritual system (see, e.g., Noddings 1984).[3] Furthermore, psychoanalysis has so far developed no robust theory of help, arguably the most obvious overarching construct under which its activities fall.

Look, help is a sometimes valuable, sometimes damaging aspect of personal, familial, and social life. If help is not typically conceived of as a moral law, it is at least partly because it is so profoundly context-dependent. But if help is not a moral law, does it need such footing to be worth considering? Or, is it the case that what many (but not all) philosophers would call the "gratuitousness" of help (Strawson 1986, 84–120; Watson 1996) is its most obvious attribute and its greatest virtue.[4] What if help were not a "virtue"? What if help were not an intersubjective ideal? Isn't help enough?

---

2   It is not.

3   I think we are all aware of the word used to describe Eve: *ezer,* עֵזֶר. It means helper, helpmate, and helpmeet, which are all the same. Some apologists argue that this is not as sexist and misogynistic as it sounds, because God is said to provide help and to be a helper in other parts of the Bible (Psalm 115:9: "O Israel, trust in the Lord! He is their help and their shield"). I don't know about this.

4   I hesitate, of course, to use the term "virtue," because it is in "virtue ethics" that care and caring have taken on such widespread dimension and propose extensive moral responsibilities that often exceed what is reasonable.

§

"Help" is defined, by those who specialize in the subject, as "volitional behavior directed at another person that benefits a person in need without expectation for a contingent or tangible return" (Nadler 2020, 5). At once, we remark help's putatively altruistic aspect ("without expectation for a contingent or tangible return") and worry that such a definition might exclude those in "helping professions," such as teachers, therapists, or nurses. Indeed, bankers and machine-workers may also be said to help others. At the same time, all of these people receive returns, however tangible, from their activities. Here I speak not only of income garnered — which is not inconsiderable — but of feelings of self-esteem and other "psychic income" derived from work.[5]

The essential question is the end of our poursuite, the ensuite of our pourquoi. In the mind, imagined answers, shaped like answers, forgotten dreams that never touch our innermost distraught, rehearse a former thought, an image, a nostalgia, a mistake of beauty. Even if tonight we say pourquoi, tomorrow we awake to follow our former selves. Of course, the poursuite has then mishappened, misshapen as it was by inessential questions that neglect what we do, what we do it for, why we lie about our reasons. It must give us pause, the enormity of our monstrous task. Sometimes sublimations multiply. Shaped like purposes, the remains of yesterpurposes remain, translate themselves into purposes repeated, recreate our former selves and former selves. Old heroes, buried without pomp at hills' bottoms, mortally rejoice. They remain the centers of themselves. Today's researchers expurgate old answers. The work is once again undone.

While we tend to think of help as largely instrumental or pragmatic — as in the giving of instruction, tools, or assistance to make another's task easier — for the child, help includes these

---

5   … or derived (possibly) from being helpful.

activities but finds its true benefits on the (facilitative) emotional and intellectual register. Likewise, we tend to think of help synchronically (at one time-point) and without regard for interpretive context, as if help occurred in a vacuum. Rather, an act of help is what Gergen and Gergen call merely "an integer in an interpretive system." Indeed, help has been mistakenly "accepted as an event in nature [which] is shown to have no existence independent of a meaning system" (1983, 144). Help is not, therefore, an "objective occurrence" whereby we can determine its helping aspect by observing the "precise character of the action" (144–45).[6]

So, we must combine two inadequate definitions to arrive at a more suitable one. Help requires the establishment of an *interpretive context* or *system of meaning* — a relationship, in several senses — in which help does not threaten the creativity, autonomy, or personhood of the helpee and in which, instead, help facilitates development and strengthens the self. This is a creative act.

§

Let us say there are two poles of help, along a sort of continuum:

1. Instrumental help offered or given directly such that the occurrence of help within almost any interpretive context or system of meaning will render it temporary (but not necessarily trivial), e.g., fetching a toy on a high shelf; and

2. Help that strengthens the helpee's self because it can be readily internalized as a good (helping) object, e.g., helping a child develop a new skill, which may even involve the withholding of help at times.

---

6 There are contexts and relationships in which it may be helpful to shoot someone.

In the latter case, help is given in a facilitative context that privileges the facilitative function of help over the instrumental.

Help presents a dilemma, for it begins from a place of incomplete autonomy, of insufficiency, and it asks that a helper step in either to gratify a need, or to help the nascent person come into himself, so that he can become an adult who needs less and less help. Thus, there is reason to suspect that ambivalence, resentment, envy, and even hatred may be built into our need for help. To resolve this dilemma — which involves, among other things, integrating the experience of being helped — is to acknowledge one's incompleteness and vulnerability within certain limits, which can only happen as the child matures.

Once again, help must be given in an interpretive context or system of meaning that does not threaten the creativity, autonomy, or personhood of the helpee. Helpees may feel their autonomy under attack in environments rich in certain forms of help, particularly those that lean toward the first pole of instrumental help. Worse, help may threaten to take 'something important away' from helpees in contexts where help takes on the meaning of supporting those who have failed to achieve autonomy, which threatens humiliation and feelings of dependence, inadequacy, indebtedness, inequity, and even exploitation (Hatfield and Sprecher 1983, 128–31).[7]

Alternatively, help may be given in such a way that it invites helpees to develop themselves. The statement sounds Winnicottian for a reason. Help can be a transitional function. Help opens up "an intermediate area of experiencing" that lies between the inner and outer worlds (Winnicott 1953). Such help is given in an interpretive context or system of meaning in which the helpee's experience is one of internal fortification that is nonetheless sponsored by another.

---

7   In a well-known study, people who perceived the United States as an imperialist power were far more averse to receiving aid than those who did not view the US in this way. In this case, "recipients viewed the assistance as a manipulative ploy intended to reinforce American world dominance" (Gergen and Gergen 1974).

The interpretive context in which these two conditions are met, where help is given freely and does not intrude upon the recipient's creativity, autonomy, or personhood, and where helping persons and things take on the meaning of strengthening the self is, for the child, the transitional context of *play*. Something of this playful experience, we may hope, will be carried over into adult experience as a capacity to give and take with others without undue threats to the self.

§

In most forms of help, the needs of the helper are, in fact, subordinated to the needs of the helpee. Although this may not be fully perceived or known by the helpee, it remains a crucial matter.[8] The more help occludes the subjectivity of the helper and focuses solely on the needs of the helpee, the more difficult it becomes to see how the helper's own experience is crucial in determining the kind and amount of help that will be offered.

Helpers do have their own motives, needs, purposes, and desires for returns on their emotional and psychic investments. These motives, needs, purposes, and desires, along with those of the helpee, are fitted unconsciously into what I have called an *interpretive context* or *system of meaning* in which help is offered, transmuted, or withheld. The terms, boundaries, and nature of this interpretive context are, ideally, creative, interactive, and negotiated.[9]

---

8   The young child, for instance, is largely blind to the sacrifices parents make on his behalf. Whether the helpee be a child or an adult, feelings of *ressentiment,* discussed above, are likely to arise in helpers, however unconsciously.

9   Developmentally, all this is appropriate so long as one considers the caregiving advice given by D.W. Winnicott: "adaptation with a gradual reduction of adaptation" (1989, 146). The reduction of adaptation is necessary so that there is room for the child to develop independence and to recognize the subjectivities of others. This is not to say that the disruptions of primary narcissism, omnipotence, or creativity, along with the confrontation with the Reality Principle, are not shocks.

Let me say more about what an interpretive context or system of meaning might be. I have nothing to add to the many
branches of philosophy and cognitive science that contend seriously with this matter. All I want to note is that we come to
know the world (and ourselves) by a process of discovery, of
discovering what was once unknown and integrating it into our
experience as best we can.

As Peter Marris writes in *Loss and Change* (1986), for the
child (and the adult), "each discovery is the basis for the next, in
a series of interpretations which gradually consolidate […] into
an understanding of life" (8). Because the interpretive contexts
and systems of meaning we develop come to serve as the structure of our very understanding, we relinquish them only with
great resistance, for without them, "we would be *helpless*" to get
along in the world (8, emphasis added).

Indeed, it is our investment in our interpretive contexts and
systems of meaning that lies at the heart of what Marris calls
the "conservative impulse" (8), which concerns not political
but philosophical and psychological conservatism. "It does not
matter," of course, "that the system may be false on another system's terms, so long as it identifies experiences in a way which
enables people to attach meaning to them and respond" (7).[10]
This holds true even (or, in some cases especially) for a system
of meaning that predominantly features loss, anxiety, shame, or
helplessness.[11]

The helplessness we feel when faced with a dislocation of
sense and meaning is mirrored in early growing-up experience.
Regardless of whether we conceive of early childhood behav-

---

10 It is to say that the truth or falsity, reasonableness or unreasonableness of
    someone's interpretive context or system of meaning, is not at issue in part
    because these are "givens" within the contexts and systems, which is al-
    most reminiscent of Thomas Kuhn's reasoning in the *Structure of Scientific
    Revolutions* (1962), by which we are always locked into a paradigm by the
    terms of the paradigm itself.

11 Contra Camus who mistakenly declares "helplessness" to have no place
    in the absurd "reasoning" he expounds in *The Myth of Sisyphus* (1991) (see
    "Sisyphus Doesn't Want Your Help," this volume).

ior as the result of drives or of relationships with internal and external objects, a child's smile or cry ought to be heard and responded to in a context of predictability, stability, and regularity. Help is needed less and less the more the child is capable of internalizing the helping functions of parents. The reliably and appropriately helped child can then develop *internal (helping) good objects* that stabilize and strengthen his ego.

§

I'd like to continue by talking about the idea of givenness in relation to what I regard as the ultimate project of maturation: coming into oneself.

What is given is immutable. Its presence and function are inscrutable. It is *just* there.

The hotel is warm but the world is cold. You walk faubourgs and faubourgs. They say Paris is an escargot: îles, rives, numéros. To-morrow's orphaned industries engulf the ancien régime. The world subsumes itself transparently. You sit in a small October park, where, for weeks, the carousel has stopped. After long waiting, some people arrive at the park. You imagine them to be orphans. You are not an orphan. You have never known an orphan. You are merely adjectives: large, warm, immoderate. Your orphans are your adjectives. Your imagination of orphans is related to your quality of having qualities like these. Everything reculminates yestermomenta. The angels won't help you. The people in the park are tired, all of us perhaps watching indefatigable imaginary orphans run circles around the stopped carousel. The world is no longer enough in its not-enoughness. Your impoverished hallucinations of orphans are proof that the world is not enough, and yet, it seems to be enough to live, even without enough. Nevertheless, you believe there must be a more satisfying way of being dissatisfied. Once, you said nothing should ever be stopped. Not carousels, criminals, habits. You moved, needing none of yourself. Stopping took strength. Living while stopped took too much. Stopping the self took the whole self, and more. So now you are certain, even or especially in October, even in hotels, even in Parisian gris, that "the hotel is all: à la fin tu es là." In the end, there you are. The carousel was covered with dead leaves. Kids smoked by it. It wasn't special. All the same, for a moment (when, exactly, you can't say) your orphans spun circles around the dead carousel, riding horses, eyes full of lights, making their own spectacular music.

Until the child can help himself, parents present items, projects, meanings, and purposes to the child in an orderly way so that they are aligned with the child's wishes or needs. This turns out to be a goodly share of parental helping.

In normal early childhood experience, the child reaches out into the world and creates whatever he finds because of such help by parents. This is a paradox of Winnicott's:

> At first whatever object gains a relationship with the infant is created by the infant […]. It is like an hallucination […]. Obviously the way the mother or her substitute behaves is of paramount importance here. One mother is good and another bad at letting a real object be just where the infant is hallucinating an object so that in fact the infant gains the illusion that the world can be created and that what is created is the world. (1989, 53)

Objects (both physical objects and objects as in others, in an object-relations sense) are there, but they are not *just* there in that they are not experienced as immovable givens. They are created and used by the healthy child. And, of course, it begins as a fantasy but becomes true in adulthood that "the world can be created" and "what is created is the world."

The child who comes into himself can discover, create, destroy, and re-fashion objects on the world on his own terms, which is to say, in accordance with his own imagination. All this is accomplished by no small effort on the part of parents who hold, handle, present, and otherwise manipulate the environment so that the child meets with success in his efforts.

Without such help, the child's reality would be utterly *given* — which is not to suggest it may not also be chaotic or inscrutable — in the sense of being *only already there,* like a plaster for the child to fit himself into, that is, to adapt to.

Instead, the parent allows the infant "to have the illusion that objects in external reality can be real to the infant, that is to say that they can be hallucinations since it is only hallucinations that feel real. If an external object is to seem real then the relationship to it must be that of a relationship to an hallucination" (Winnicott 1989, 54).[12]

Coming into oneself refers to the multifaceted process of creating and integrating elements of the self and world.[13] I use the phrase *coming into oneself,* because there are any number of things one may become instead of oneself (e.g., a 'given' self, a false self, a psychotic self, etc.), and because coming into oneself is experienced as if the self were *always already there.*

This state of already-being-real is ideal for young children who very much need their own existence to be a (the) primary *given* thing in their worlds. Alternatively, a false self may be "given" to the child such that only while inhabiting that false self does the child exist and receive help. Thus, coming into oneself begins with an interpretive context or system of meaning in which the self's reality is the central "given" in the child's world.

At the same time that the child is learning to make the subjective objective, he is taking in aspects of the world around him

---

12 On the self-strengthening nature of this sort of transitional experience: "This quartet is not just an external fact produced by Beethoven and played by the musicians; and it is not my dream, which as a matter of fact would not have been so good. The experience, coupled with my preparation of myself for it, enables me to create a glorious fact. I enjoy it because I say I created it, I hallucinated it, and it is real and would have been there even if I had been neither conceived or not conceived" (Winnicott 1989, 58).

13 Of course, the self and world are never fully distinguishable, and are even more intertwined for the child, yet the (lifelong) process of sorting out what belongs inside and what belongs outside, what is part of the self and what is part of the not-self, begins in development and ends in the achievement of (relative) autonomy, freedom, efficacity, and selfhood.

(i.e., his relationships with parents and others) as internal objects that shape his internal landscape. The child must also "take in" the capacity to filter or reject elements of the external world. The establishment of a boundary is necessary for the development of autonomy, for without a boundary between inside and outside, the child would be unable to hold onto his inner experience and to act from a place of core self-feeling (see Shengold 1989; Levine 2003, 60–61). This boundary, too, must not be inflexible or impermeable, but must be a "given."

Persons *come into themselves* when needs are met and when expressions and actions arise not as reactions to givens but as feelings of living and inner worth, as core sensations of being, or as what R.D. Laing calls "ontological security" (1969). These expressions and actions must have meaningful effects on the world outside lest the world be construed as impossibly given, and the child's will be construed as impotent or non-existent.

If the child is prevented from creating his world because help is either lacking or always intruding, the child is left with a given or ready-made world (of whatever nature and imbued with however much helpfulness), seemingly a world in which to play but, effectively, a dead world where creativity and play are impossible, because the child is made psychically inactive or lifeless in his encounters with help.

Help-specialists call this a "threat to autonomy and self-esteem" (Fisher, Nadler, and DePaulo 1983), where impinging help defeats attempts to achieve autonomy or independence, and this negative outcome is accentuated in childhood experience. Where there is unneeded or impinging help, the child becomes helpless to achieve agency and will; that is, to learn to achieve his own ends.

To say the child develops the ability to achieve his own ends is to say that he has a will. Parents develop the child's will through countless daily activities in which they help the child make his desire real, from preparing a meal to lending a hand in building a block castle. Giving objects a nudge and celebrating small achievements belong to helping the child develop a will because, under ideal conditions and with appropriate help, the growing child experiences the power of making the psychical real and the possible (e.g., desired, gratifying, wished-for) actual as his own.[14]

The desire to rediscover in adult experience what was "given" in the child's experience is something shared by all of us.[15] It is the fundamental interpretive context and system of meaning to which we have been given. In addition to being deeply familiar, it has stood in for the satisfaction of true needs and desires long enough that it is the only reliable substitute.

§

At its best, help is transitional, as our experience allows us to resist the desire to "lose or fuse" (Lewin and Schultz 1992), to become one with the other or to hermetically seal the door between the self and the other. Alternatively, care can collapse transitional space with selfishness, selflessness, or the sheer weight of desire.

Help includes warmth, attention, kindness, assistance, and support. It consists in virtually everything the parent does for the child: facilitate, manage, assist, hold, etc. Of course, these functions must change and adapt to the child from infancy through adolescence. Such help is part of the child's and parents' system of relatedness, which is the primary interpretive context or system of meaning in which the child develops. Parents may fail to help children because they mistakenly believe that their care is enough. Alternatively, failures of help comprise parental behaviors that more patently fail to meet the child's true needs,

---

14 "Helping oneself" implies that there are things within the self that are stronger than the self. These are internal helpers created in the image of a relatively consistent helping other. The result is a helpful — as opposed to harsh or unforgiving — internal environment of which the self may make use by integrating help offered by others into his own intentions and purposes.

15 See "Children in a Helpless World," this volume.

including neglect, an absence of attunement, abandonment, impingement, and abuse.

Perhaps the most crucial form of help throughout maturation lies in the reliable good nature of the parent in times of the child's distress, allowing the child to borrow from, partake in, and internalize qualities of the caregiver's stronger and more capacious psyche. There is an element of "absorbing the blow" or "taking the bullet" in all of this. The parent must neutralize the threatening and toxic emotions for the sake of the child. But at least the parent is together with the child through his or her period of anguish.

This togetherness proves to be an important theoretical matter concerning the transitional experience of helping and being helped. Helping while "together" (and not helping while unified or fused) means that the child is not alone but, at the same time, has enough space to take in help and make it his own.[16] Failures of help, of course, damage children's ability to internalize parents as good (helping) objects, needed to develop the relative independence we associate with selfhood. And, as we have just seen, where there is unneeded or impinging help, the self is at risk of being proven worthless, as help in this context implies a failure to achieve autonomy or independence, and only reaffirms the need to assume a false-self posture.[17]

Of course, if the parent is unwilling or unable to perform helping functions — perhaps because the parent's own world is dangerously unsafe and, in that sense, no stronger than the child's — then the child is forsaken, *helpless*.

---

16 Perhaps this will not be understood.

17 At the same time, it hardly needs to be stated that failures of help — as in failures of attention, object-presentation, handling, and holding — while potentially devastating, are both inevitable and necessary parts of development. If help were perfectly and completely given and received, children would never grow up.

§

To fully understand failures of help, first we must recall that the child occupies a vulnerable position in several senses. At the most basic level, the child is physically helpless amidst a world of adults. Help begins early, in the very first moments of the child's life, from a place of tremendous need and dependence, and it asks a helper to gratify its needs and desires. Children do not have the power to determine the course of their own daily lives, and depend, to a great degree, on the help of others to live.

At a psychic level, the same is true, but its meaning runs deeper. The need for togetherness on the part of the child cannot be overestimated. Lack of togetherness with parents leaves children vulnerable to feeling helpless in an unhelpful world. As the child relies on helpful, benevolent others for help, if those others are inadequate, deficient, or absent (even in an emotional if not literal sense), then the child, who has not yet developed the psychic means of helping himself, inhabits a world without help: a helpless world.

In a helpless world, we have no means of feeling safe from threatening, fearsome, aggressive, or destructive impulses and fantasies, arising from within or without. Unreliable or missing experiences of help suggest that we are alone in facing such dangers albeit without the necessary internal resources to "help ourselves."

In helpless moments, the child's self is unable to obtain what it needs and finds its fantasy of narcissistic omnipotence disrupted by an unwelcome sense of destruction and desolation. If such moments are numerous or severe enough, they become permanent features of the growing child's psyche, destroying his ability to come into himself. Lack of appropriate help precludes the internalization of what John Bowlby and attachment theorists call an "internal working model" of the world as a place where the self can exercise its will, making possible (e.g., desired, gratifying, wished-for) experience actual.

Of course, help can go wrong in too many ways to enumerate. It can be deficient or inadequate, as in neglect or lack of affection. It can be misdirected toward a false self, at the expense of the true self's needs, as in many forms of abuse, where there is love and care but *not the kind of love and care the child needs.* It can be *impinging,* disturbing our ability to discover and create our own experience. It would be laborious to have to separate these three sub-categories in discussing these complex matters, so I trust the reader will understand terms like "failure of help" or "inadequate help" as referring to one or more of them, *selon le cas.*[18]

§

Karen Horney goes so far as to refer to the lack of help and care as "the basic evil" (1937, 80), although this comment is made rather casually and holds the potential to be taken out of context.[19] That such failures of appropriate help are "evil" is not to say that the child has a sophisticated concept (or any concept at all) of evil.[20] Rather, it means simply that child who grows up in an unhelpful context has suffered a trauma, a break in the child's

---

18 A great failure is the failure to help the child cope with hate, and especially with the conflict associated with hating and loving the parent or parents. This is far more complex than basic ambivalence or the integration of part-objects into whole objects. The child who has a parent who fails to help may hate that parent for failing him. Even the child who has a parent who does *not* fail him and *does* contain the child's hate, if we believe Wilfred Bion, may hate that parent out of envy for his or her strength (see "Attacks on Help," this volume). If, for whatever reason, the child hates his parent, or even if the child is merely unable to process hate because the channels of communication with the parent have been obscured or complicated, the child will be unable to internalize aliveness, help, and benignity from his parent and to use them to construct a lively and healthy inner world.

19 Horney went on to argue that this basic evil led to "basic anxiety" as well as a three-tiered schema of neurotic defenses, owing to the child's inability to express rage at needed helpers (1937).

20 William James (1911, 162–63) argued that it was "not the conception or intellectual perception of evil, but the grisly blood-freezing heart palsying sensation of it close upon one, and no other conception or sensation able to live for a moment in its presence. How irreverently remote seem all our usual refined optimisms and intellectual and moral consolations in the

togetherness with his caregivers, on which his survival depends. For Winnicott, failures of appropriate help are *traumata* for the child precisely because the caregiver "breaks faith" and so breaks the relationship and the interpretive context established in the family as they had been known thus far (1989, 146).

Failures and impingements of help may lock the growing individual in an untenable or false posture. A parent may offer what might be referred to as "false help," where help addresses intolerable experience on the part of caregiver or in some way attends to an idea of what the child should be, rather than who the child is. In this interpretive context or system of meaning, the offer of help would carry the meaning of making the child *other* than himself. Of course, child abuse, in all of its forms (emotional, physical, sexual, verbal), reflects complex but terribly damaging interpretive contexts in which the child is "helped" — as in the giving of attention or relation, even in a conflictual way — only to the extent that he can be treated as if he were an adult capable of coping with lust, dismissal, derision, or hate.

Seemingly helpful treatment by parents may also be aimed at yielding tangible returns in the form of, say, a cessation of unpleasant behavior by the child. Help of this nature is not aimed at assisting the child work through, say, an experience of frustration, but, rather, at ensuring that the child stops crying. Within this interpretive context, help holds the meaning of repressing genuine (displays of) negative emotions by the child. Failed or inappropriate help of this kind forces the child to develop a false self in order to receive help and achieve togetherness with caregivers.[21]

Children try to please their parents, and, often, children help their parents, even if not obviously. Since the child should not be the helper but the helpee, it is typical in such circumstances for

---

presence of a need of help like this. Here is the real core of the religious problem: Help! Help!"

21 The false self is "false" not because there are given (true and false) essences within each person, but because it exists for the sake of, to please, or to help others.

the self to fail to come into itself, and, rather, to develop a false self organized around powerful impulses to seek (false) help, on one hand, and, on the other, rage at the experience of helplessness in an unhelpful world the child's real self feels.

Those who do not receive help in predictable, regular ways develop shame instead of self-worth. The unanswered cry and the part of the self that needs help are *disconfirmed* by the parent's neglect.[22] The needs that cry out for help but receive none readily turn into abjected aspects of the self, parts of the self so repugnant that they do not deserve help or attention. The child's experience of helplessness thus turns into an experience of *worthlessness* — "*I do not deserve help*" — if help is not received reliably, in time, and in good enough measure. Worthlessness, along with attendant anxiety and depression, then, may be understood in terms of shame created by helplessness.

§

"People help because they care" is perhaps the most widely held belief about the causes and correlates of helping. It is known as the "empathy-altruism hypothesis," which holds that "helping is motivated by genuine concern with the other's welfare" (Nadler 2020, 76). This hypothesis (see Batson 2011; Keltner et al. 2014) has been questioned of late by new research in social psychology.[23]

One important study (Smith, Keating, and Stotland 1989) found that, when primed to feel an empathic connection with another subject, participants helped others if they could receive

---

22 "Disconfirmation" is a Laingian term (1961), meaning non-recognition to the point of erasure in a relationship or exchange. Confirmation is an ideal of seeing the whole person. Disconfirmation means negating, through inattention or rejection, a part of the other's self such that the other feels that it does not or should not exist.

23 What is unquestionable is that conflating help with care makes it more difficult to understand both; on the other hand, the statement above is, for many, an analytic truth, since, for them, caring is helping and vice versa.

feedback about the importance of their help. This experiment, rather than supporting a hypothesis organized around empathy, seems to suggest that helping is based on a selfish motivation to receive positive feedback, praise, or prestige as a result of helping behavior.

It may even be that "giving to others constitutes 'costly signaling' that tells the recipient and others that the helper is resourceful enough to bear the short-term costs of helping others" (Nadler 2020, 81), and this "self-sacrifice might actually be self-presentation" (Van Vugt and Hardy 2010, 108). Here, "people helped not because they were motivated to relieve the other's predicament but because they sought to aggrandize themselves in the eyes of others" (Nadler 2020, 82).

These explanations all fall under the heading of egoistic motivations, which hold that help is given largely to increase social and psychological inequality between the helper and helpee: "to gain prestige, people compete over who will be more generous, given that the helpful act is visible or knowable to other group members" (Nadler 2020, 81).

A related explanation is offered by Aronfreed (1968), who argued that many children learn to experience happiness when they relieve *others'* distress. That is, the child experiences a "vicarious joy" when, for instance, he helps a parent (Nadler 2020, 77). Here, in a relationship that is distressingly upside-down, the child is the helper and the child's vicarious joy at helping the parent "forms the basis for adult helping that is motivated by helpers' anticipated vicarious joy" (77). In this case, the false self of the child, developed in the pattern of pleasing others to experience joy, may one day offer help as an adult, even if for tragic reasons.

While most research has focused on the relation between help and belongingness, Maner et al. (2002) found that helping increased the feeling of "oneness" between observer and helpee, suggesting that helping the other "is akin to helping oneself" (Nadler 2020, 78).

It remains true that in almost every instance, the motivation for helping (whether it is belongingness, status, or oneness) has to do with the relationship between helper and helpee as well as the interpretive context or system of meaning in which help is given. It would seem that the helper either wishes to become close to (or become "one with") the helpee or the helper wishes to improve his status and prestige vis-à-vis the social group, or both.

As Nadler (2020, 79) observes, "posing the question [about the drivers of helpful behavior] in this binary form obscures the fact that benefitting oneself and the needy need not be mutually exclusive." That is true, and the feeling of "oneness" during an act of help need not be disparaged as a merely egoistic or selfish intention.[24] What I think is being alluded to here, perhaps a bit clumsily, is the *transitional work* of help.

Help means taking on some of the burden of the other, even if only for a while, maybe even for an instant. This is not merger or fusion. Nor is it the desire to belong to a social group or to improve one's standing in that group. I have called it "togetherness." As opposed to seeing the other as an object of identification, or as a competitor in a social hierarchy, helping involves being "together" with the other, but not being the other, especially in moments of need, lack, or pain.

§

Research on helping motivations has "ping-ponged" between egoism and altruism since the 1980s with little resolution (Nadler 2020, 78). There are equity theories, reactance theories, attribution theories, threat-to-self-esteem theories, and more.[25]

Nevertheless, "on the positive side," Nadler (2020, 97–101) argues: "Help has an instrumental benefit of ameliorating the recipient's difficulties and it can also be a psychologically sup-

---

24 Indeed, it is, at the very least, awkward to call a desire for merger or fusion *ego*istic.

25 It's a bit boring.

portive experience that constitutes a sign of the helper's genuine care for one's well-being."

Here, help reveals the presence of care: a problematic assumption on many counts. First, it is not clear what interpretive devices are in play when one is deciphering what help has been given and whether it qualifies the helper as a caregiver. Furthermore, as we know, help may be misused such that it does not reflect genuine help or care. Finally, there are situations in which care, like help, can create feelings of inadequacy, excessive obligation, or exploitation on the part of the helpee, meaning that others' care is not a *universally* "psychologically supportive experience."

There seem to be four major dangers faced by recipients of help: (1) inconsistency in the helpee's value of self-reliance; (2) negative social comparison between the capacious helper and the needy helpee; (3) feelings of indebtedness to the helper that "limit one's freedom of action"; and (4) reactance, which may be defined as an experience or expectation of a threat or loss of freedom.

What we can say is that negative feelings like indebtedness are "associated with the recipient's desire to erase a debt that he or she owes the benefactor. Until this debt has been repaid, recipients seek to keep their distance from the helper" (Nadler 2020, 102), for if "being helped takes on the meaning of becoming indebted to benefactors," it results in "loss of freedom and the aversive emotion of reactance" (Nadler 2020, 97; see also Greenberg 1980; Brehm 1989).[26]

The most influential factor in generating helping behavior and in the positive receipt of help appears to be the interpretive context or system of meaning in which help was given. Relationships of help among adults will be organized around each adult's growing-up experiences as well as the present (cultural, social, political, etc.) contexts of their interactions. To take the long

---

26 In fact, in a seminal work, Heider (1958) found that, to the extent that the helper expected or obliged the helpee to be grateful, the less gratitude was to be expected.

view, those who are fortunate enough to experience transitional help are far more likely than others to "give, seek, and receive help" later in life (Nadler 2020, 106).

§

If we cannot internalize the good aspects of others, then others can be seen only as obstacles to gratification.

§

As we know, "help" refers us to a relation between both persons and within a person or self, which double-sense reveals help's central dilemma. The receipt of help risks the anxiety-piquing possibility that the recipient is not self-sufficient or has failed to overcome helplessness.

This specific anxiety is about the self's basic worth and value. If the self has no basic worth or value, it may as well be dead. A helpless self may avoid such experiences of worthlessness when given adequate help at appropriate times, but for many, helplessness and its attendant anxiety become fixtures around which life and the world are organized.

Failures of help, as in neglect, abuse, or abandonment, have the power to forever alter the child's internal environment and, thereby, the child's relation to itself. As noted above, Winnicott (1989, 145) calls a failure of help a traumatic "breaking of faith" by the parent/role model/other ("object," in the language of psychoanalysis) and its ability to provide help together with the helpee.

If help is not provided at essential moments in the child's development, then we might say that the child's discovery of its own helplessness comes too early, too suddenly, and too fully in the form of traumatically infused anxiety. It is traumatically tinged because it leaves the self defenseless without internal helpers, or, as Dori Laub might say, without the internal "other," the "thou" of every dialogic relationship, including, of course, the self's (2012, 41).

There is a powerful need to defend against such experience and a most effective means appears to be a rejection of helping relations and an individualistic, sometimes ruthless, survivalism, be it literal or figurative, about which I have already written extensively (see, e.g., Bowker 2014; Bowker 2016; Levine and Bowker 2019). Such survivalism, in a circular fashion, makes the self even more insecure, as the world becomes a place where destruction looms large and survival is always in doubt.

Images and depictions of the world of survivors may be readily found in contemporary popular and intellectual cultures (see Levine and Bowker 2019). In the threatening and depleted world of the survivor, help is offered, if at all, only at the rarest moments and at considerable risk. Help is received with comparable paranoia, for receiving help may signify the self's incompleteness or inadequacy at procuring its needs.

§

Anxiety expresses the torment of helplessness, even if it emerges in the face of evidence that external help may be (either consistently or inconsistently) available. Anxiety is infused with the dread that the self cannot survive without help, but is also filled with envy and hate of external help and helpers. At the same time, anxiety expresses guilt for the hatred aimed toward would-be helpers (see "Anxiety," this volume).

Insecure attachments to parents are those in which, to one degree or another, the reliability of help is uncertain. This uncertainty is, empirically speaking, even more damaging than the certain knowledge of the unavailability of help. Much anxiety may be understood as a consequence of a tormented or tantalized orientation to help, a presentiment of and ambivalence about helplessness and all that attends it, including the wish for help, the uncertainty of help, the desire to be free of the need for help, the worry that one does not deserve help, the envious attack on the receipt of help, and more.

The failed child and the inconsistently helped child develop splits in their psyches, schisms between the needs and hurt within the self that would benefit from help, and the very same hurt and needs abjected as shameful and intolerably bad aspects of the self, unworthy of help. The extraordinary agony of this situation leaves the self, in the language of Melanie Klein, in a paranoid-schizoid dilemma, wherein both the failure of help and the receipt of help signify the loss of the good in the self and the world.

Although we have all faced, at one time or another to some degree, failures of help, a truly *helpless world* is one in which the self can neither find help nor help itself. If such helplessness is a significant feature of growing up, then a result of a lack of help in the home or family is that the world becomes organized around help's absence. In other words, the world becomes a place where help and helpers are needed yet vilified, a place where persons and groups are marked by their (shameful) need for help or their (hateful, enviable) "privilege" in having received help.

In such a situation, a state of helplessness is actively maintained by attacking help and helpers, owing to envy and resentment, both psychically and manifestly in the outer world. Such attacks are designed to ensure that no help will be found and one's helplessness will be shared by others, even as the attacks themselves may be understood as cries for help. In the end, they repeat the experience of needing help and failing to find it.

While most have understood help as an expression of our need for "belongingness" and the aversion to helping as a marker of our drive for independence, what may be overlooked is the extent to which we may seek to belong to groups whose identities are closely aligned with helplessness itself. Such groups, which frequently include hate groups, victim groups, and survivor groups, take as their mission the rejection or destruction of helping agents, as beneficial help becomes, itself, a threat to the group's fundamental fantasy that it inhabits a cruel and unhelpful world.

If understood as a helping agent, individuals and groups may attack the government itself or its specific policies and projects, from affordable healthcare to foreign aid, or affirmative action to local, State, or Federal public health measures. Indeed, it is a tragedy of political psychology that there are just as many opportunities to give or receive help as there are opportunities to play out the internal drama of helplessness, trauma, and hate in the external world by attacking helpful policies and with institutions and organizations that offer much needed help.

The idea of "help" can be a key to understanding contemporary politics, society, and culture, as it organizes debates about trauma and witnessing, "helplessness" before the Other, bystanding and privilege, moral obligations, "what we owe each other," and more. The problem is, of course, that in civil society help must be organized not around the desire (or lack of desire) to help nor around care or love in general, but around respect for and defense of what it means to be a mature adult. In civil society, to the extent that we have a duty to help others, that duty must be derived from something other than parental or familial (or universal) love. The crisis of help and helplessness in civil society, then, is really a crisis of contradiction between the home (where help ought to be available) and the adult world, where loving is not a defining feature of relating.

In-Patient

I don't want to write about being in a mental hospital twice — twice because the first time didn't help and it took two weeks or so to find out how little it helped a lot of it is about "medication adjustment" and they do it very quickly in the hospital because if you collapse or something you're right there but when they pull you off every medication you've been taking for years all at the same time it takes a while to start going mad again or dying or feeling like you're falling forever.

Is it humiliating or exhibitionistic to write about this? yes but it is also banal.

It was not primarily a shit-on-the-walls, fights-in-the-halls type of hospital but you still couldn't leave the ward or see much of anything out of the fogged windows most people were there like me because their meds stopped working and they were freaking out I am sorry I am writing largely without punctuation it is not an affectation it is my way of keeping in touch with reality.

In the hospital everything is normal because everything is slow it is like a different world a texture covers all a mist hangs in the air covering everything and everyone everywhere the rooms and hallways are all freezing inside especially in the summertime but the texture of the place makes even crazy things seem normal.

Even before you show up you have to get your shrink to arrange it then wait then go in early the next day for intake then wait two hours in a small room filled with cloudy glass block and they'll feed you something from the cafeteria while you wait if you ask them then an hour of paperwork then you go to the ward where inevitably something is happening but nothing too severe to bring someone new onto the ward for everyone to inspect while gathered around whatever was/is happening.

The first inspection however is done in private by the nurses who make you take off all your clothes and then check your body for hidden wounds and weapons and compliment you on your tattoos and muscles it is kind of hot if you have exhibitionistic tendencies then you put your clothes back on they take your vitals the first of several times per day and see if you know who the President is and if you can keep subtracting 7 from 100 without losing count.

Maybe banality is the name of the hospital game. 93, 86, 79, 72, 65, 58…

Later you are inspected by the other patients and it is generally not hot according to Steve the bipolar psychotic government MD who was very talkative and changed his clothes several times a day "the way [I] carry myself" is somehow regal or powerful because it is what magically ousted a mysterious man named "Buffalo Bill" from the top spot in the hospital once I arrived I had no idea what he was talking about I never met or even saw Buffalo Bill I guess he stayed away from me for three days then got discharged it is true that I am a sort of big guy a little over 6 feet and about 240 because I lift weights and I wear a long beard and keep my hair almost completely shaven because I am almost bald I never thought people looked at me and thought "oh shit I better hide for three days" but then again I never thought anyone would look at me and say "hey that guy needs help" but I did I was more worried about this than about Buffalo Bill I wouldn't have hurt him or anybody and I was too weak to be the alpha but apparently I had to be because everyone hated Buffalo Bill his rule was a terror and he was said to be the craziest of them all which is exactly what Wilfred Bion says: that groups elect the craziest person as their leader what does that say about me?

I wasn't suicidal but I had had the most severe BREAKDOWN of my life (and yes I call it a breakdown because that is what it feels like) but for everyone else I was simply having:

- Major Depressive Episode
- Panic Attacks
- Generalized Anxiety
- Obsessive-Compulsive Disorder

but I was actually experiencing an eclipse of myself.

Everything was dark soot root fuck crap rot and so so so heavy that I wanted only to sleep everything shameful everything terrifying suicide thoughts crying all the time I couldn't eat or sleep or stop feeling I was going to throw up and melt into a puddle on the floor.

From my journal:

I feel that everything, everything about me has been lost, erased, I don't know who I am or what I want or need any more. I don't even know if I want to live I need to want to live but right now there is only panic terror, fear, worry, anxiety, nervousness… I am so scared that no one will truly HELP me. I feel like I am coming apart the reality I live in feels so bad and dangerous I don't know what to do… I feel so bad I don't even know where to begin. My body and mind feel bad. I feel sick inside and all over. I am very frightened for seemingly no reason I am afraid I can't function…

I think in the hospital the patients come to share each other's madnesses or at least each other's defense mechanisms to some degree or other at least if you consider how much you have to accommodate certain kinds of crazy behaviors it is easier to adopt the craziness than to undertake the behaviors without the belief that doing so is meaningful in some way I think this is oddly part of what helps about the hospital.

THE ANGELS WON'T HELP YOU

I never liked talking to anyone so much as one time a woman named Alisa who had schizophrenia and who told me very clearly yet warmly that she was upset that she heard me talking about schizophrenia and schizophrenics and wanted me to know that it is better to say "a person with schizophrenia" came back from ECT and all she could do was sing a kind of nonsense song *dee dul dee dul day* but desperately wanted to talk so we sang together in the hallways waiting for a nurse to come and take care of her "1 × 1" – nurses do 'one on one' with people who are really confused or are dangers to themselves like the girl who would just walk up to and smash her forehead on the concrete walls and cry, "I wish I had a baby!"

§

To be an in-patient is to *let in* the help of others so that you don't have to help yourself this may sound regressive but it is the kind of regression that people who are in the hospital need.

It involves a questionable breakfast every morning and they wake you up if you are sleeping so you don't miss it bed checks every ten minutes all night long balanced if not gross meals and special diets are accommodated and served normally this would be invasive and overwhelming help but here it is healthy.

The most helpful nurse in the hospital was named Jane heavily pierced and tattooed Jane came to work each day like any other, helped people, and left there was no trace of caring that would make you feel attached or guilty at the same time, all of her helpful activities were considered "normal" (in French, among other things such as *de rien* [it's nothing], one may say *c'est normal* when someone thanks you) I don't know if she cared I bet she did care but she held her caring in check somehow so that it did not interfere with the helping functions and relationships in which she was entangled on a daily basis even in conversation, she was warm and kind but kept a certain neutrality about her (see also Bowker 2018; 2019a) that I thought was more about what she could handle than anything else at first now I

54

wonder if maybe it was her way of providing better help because she was there when you needed help but didn't care about you when you didn't.

§

Was I *cared for* in the hospital? I don't know but I doubt it and, what is more, it doesn't matter I don't think that care was at all what I needed maybe even the opposite since part of the hospital experience is being free to be free to be without having to show anyone your CV free to walk around in your pyjamas free to just be a person among many in a helping setting so not only was I there because I had a breakdown on top of which my psychiatrist didn't help me change my meds but more importantly being cared for can easily become more about an inner state of the caregiver than any meaningful effect on the one cared for in this case it would have been impinging to me newly discovered freedom especially but not exclusively when one is an adult it is a bit like unconditional love in that its meaning expires in adulthood as it should.

§

My first roommate is a paranoid delusional who is so over-the-top nice he might be seriously disturbed he tells me he has a medical snoring problem but no C-Pap machine so I ask to move my cot foam mattress that is covered with the same material they use to cover gymnastics mats to the small dusty library with only one shelf of old self-help books and I sleep on the floor alternating between my own copy of the *Tao Te Ching* and a Bible that an evangelical nurse gave me my second time there I ask for a private room and am miraculously given one everything feels very spiritual now and I am praying for the first time in a long time and I feel that it is meaningful which has been a very very long time.

What were my insides doing while there? Were they healing? Were they being helped? Everything felt more stagnant as
if one were merely marking time until you could convince your
psychiatrist to release you you could always release yourself by
filing some form that got you out in 48 hours I think but this
was the more acceptable way to go. Kathy Acker says:

> You, this thing you call 'you,' was a ball turning and turning
> in the blackness only the blackness wasn't something — like
> 'black' — and it wasn't nothingness 'cause nothingness was
> somethingness. The whole thing turns up into a ball, the
> ball's ephemeral, and where are you? Your self is a ball turn-
> ing and turning as if it's being thrown from one hand to the
> other hand and every time the ball turns over you feel all
> your characteristics, your identities, slip around so you go
> crazy. When the ball doesn't turn, you feel stable. (1978, 55)

§

Let me tell you what a major depressive episode (combined with
panic disorder) feels like. Your death is immanent but that is the
least of your concerns you welcome it and hope for it to arrive it
is a fate worse than death a kind of slow torture of every nerve
before the eyes the world crumbles up and turns to disgusting
shit everything you think feel and say is vomit. You vomit everything up all the time and eat the shit of the world until it becomes you vomiting shit in an endless cycle.

§

Quickly you learn that almost everything in the hospital is help
help help. You have to get help to get your toothbrush or take a
shower. Everything is under lock and key. You have to get help
to get a pen or a Q-tip to clean your ears with (or gauge some-

one's eye out with) they cut all the strings off everything you have and shoelaces and belts are not allowed and the cords to the phones are only six inches long so there a lot of people shuffling around holding up their pants and shouting into a receiver at the same time the help runs only so deep the so-called therapists are MSW students from some nearby shit university and are there mainly to check on you and report to your doctor whether you have behaved like an average predictable patient or not.

People are bounced around to and from doctors each seemingly with a very specific agenda to which the patient must fit one likes to prescribe shock therapy I had this doctor the first time and he took me off all my meds except clonazepam and sent me in for ECT I got knocked out and when I woke apparently the first thing I said was "I can't remember my daughter's birthday" this temporary and terrifying lesion in my memory which was distressing enough to me to quit ECT was attributed to my "anxiety" for which there was nothing that could help but adding Buspirone HCL which is a fucking joke and doesn't help and makes you dizzy.[1]

§

Cliff was a 29-year-old man who for some reason had brought no clothes to change into and didn't get a delivery for some time his tank top was dirty and his pants were torn and he only had

---

[1] If you wanted to psychoanalyze this you would say that it reflected some guilt on my part for being the one getting help instead of the one giving help to my daughter and, indeed, of removing a source of help from our home for the duration of my stay in the hospital. My child lives not in a helpless world, yet it is interesting how closely she can return to it when she is not helped. She still asks me to put toothpaste on her toothbrush even though she is perfectly capable of doing this herself. What she is seeking is, at its most basic level, help, but what she really wants is for the experience of brushing her teeth to be an experience of helpful togetherness, where the instrumental help is trivial but the facilitative help (brushing teeth means a transition into day or into night, etc.) is substantial. If I refuse or suggest that she do it by herself, she gets very upset.

the socks they give out at the front desk with the little sticky strips on the bottom he looked about 18 and lived with his father in his childhood home and worked the same job he had since he was in high school and never had sex and never went to college and never got married and never traveled all this was not done out of lack of means but rather out of lack of will.

Cliff was convinced that he needed to be in lifelong in-patent hospitalization and yet was very concerned about his ability to resign himself to a life of hospitalization he insisted upon this even though the more he insisted the more they crammed him full of pills Cliff was fairly calm about everything until they told him that he did not meet the criteria of a person needing long-term psychiatric care and Cliff got furious with the nurse who told him he said "How can someone else say what I need? I'm the one who knows!"

Cliff was gently helped by being reminded to breathe which was sort of the first line of defense against real communication by the mental health care workers if you have a problem they interrupt you immediately and tell you to stop and breathe which is infantilizing and infuriating.

What is it to go mad anyway? What is it really? Does anyone know? Can anyone know? If anyone knew could he or she explain it in language? Is it the loss of connection with reality or the loss of connection with the self? Or both? For me it was the loss of connection with myself that made it impossible to move forward in reality. How do you help a person who has lost connection with himself? The best you can do is try to get him to eat and sleep and take away sharp objects? It is ludicrous but it is also weirdly adequate.

What is not helpful is the excruciating boredom no one realizes that boredom is or can be a form of severe psychic distress literally people are coloring in coloring books and watching the Lifetime channel all day long and there is nowhere to go but you are not supposed to be holed up in your room you are supposed to go to meetings like MEN'S GROUP which sounds very enticing because I believe I will be able to talk about what it is like to be an INSANE MAN in a GROUP but it is actually a short skinny guy with khakis and zero interest in group therapy reading from a worksheet and talking for 45 minutes straight about mindfulness.

So you mainly walk the corridors back and forth and left and right for hours shuffling along with your hands behind your back sometimes talking with Cliff or others who walk with you sometimes silently somehow feeling that walking in this way perhaps because it was the thing we could do that most represented action and agency made us human again and the nurses couldn't bother us to get a vitals check while walking and we were sort of above and outside of the hospital floating around at our monastic pace.

Children in a Helpless World

I.

Things begin badly when in the first paragraph of Kathy Acker's *Blood and Guts in High School* (1978) we are introduced to ten-year-old Janey and her father, Johnny, on whom Janey depended for "everything" and whom she "regarded […] as a boyfriend, brother, sister, money, amusement, and father" (7).

It turns out the two have a torrid sexual and romantic relationship that includes frank discussions of sex as well as fights about Janey's jealousy of Johnny's other girlfriends.

In spite of this, what really distresses Janey is the way that her father's help has vanished. Janey accuses him of not "helping me the way you usually do when I'm sick" (9) and tells their mutual friend that she's been "very sick" with "Pelvic Inflammatory Disease" and that "usually, Johnny helps out when I am [sick], this time he hasn't" (11). This help becomes symbolic of real parental love and not sexual abuse. Its absence means Johnny's relating to Janey as a *real child* is over. This is a *(the)* loss from which Janey cannot recover.

The plot: Janey is abused abused abused abused first her father then gang members and various brutal lovers Mr Linker sex slave traders and even Jean Genet (although she begins to love being abused and is never loved by Genet — yes, that *Jean Genet) until she gets cancer and goes blind and dies.*

No one in Janey's life helps her. Some care for her, but always the kind of caring that she does not need: the care that hurts.

The first question is whether the problem is the latest woman, Sally, who is taking up all of Johnny's energy or if it is something else. It seems clear that it is the latter, the worst thing, that Johnny no longer wants to be related to Janey in both senses: (a) of being her family relation; and (b) of relating with her. He does not want (he has never wanted) to relate with her as a daughter and has only related to her as a sexual object, which means to interact with her in an abusive manner while destroying her interpersonal boundaries and sense of self.

So, here, a lack of help is equated with a glaring sexual violation. No-help is like a rape for Janey, who will later fantasize about being raped and will even be sold into sex slavery. But, in the beginning, what she loses — what loss sets her life on its course — is help. After the two separate, their conversations are almost exclusively about monetary help and are, Janey hopes, without emotion, but of course they are not.

Johnny is fed up with Janey and puts her in an American school in New York "to make sure she doesn't return to Merida." Of course Janey is now "desperate to find the love that he had taken away from me" (31), and therefore, "I hated myself. I did everything I could to hurt myself" (32). This involves:

Every day a sharp tool, a powerful destroyer, is necessary to cut away dullness, lobotomy, buzzing, belief in human beings, stagnancy, images, and accumulation. As soon as we stop believing in human beings, rather know we are dogs and trees, we'll start to be happy. […] We must go farther and become crazier." (37)

In her discussion of an abortion (which immediately follows her remark about hurting herself), Janey feels that "having an abortion was obviously just like getting fucked. If we closed our eyes and spread our legs, we'd be taken care of. […] I love it when men take care of me. […] I got to like that pale green room, the women who were more scared than I was so I could comfort them, the feeling someone was taking care of me. I felt more secure there than in the outside world. I wanted a permanent abortion" (33).

Janey is in lifelong bondage to her father due to his gross sexual and emotional abuse. She imagines freedom but because she is inwardly traumatized and enraged, engendering both a deep longing for care and a ferocious kind of wildness meaning she can never separate or distinguish her desire to be from her desire to harm and to destroy.

Living needed teeth. If we drank we drank the desperation of the day, the father, the sun, reddened our backs, apologized in weakness and wanted for strength but mainly woke up wary, wandered into the funny fields, windless as they were, and felt surprisingly alone.

For Janey, love and crime are intertwined, for she really does not know love that is separate from harm, only abuse combined with her own desire and need. She has rejected her own desires and needs and has transformed them into sources of shame, the destructive energy of which means that love leads to violence and crime with Tommy, also a member of the street gang to which Janey belongs, the Scorpions:

Love turned me back to crime. Tommy and I kidnapped children. Smeared up the walls of buildings. Carried dangerous weapons and used them. Did everything we could to dull our judgment and acted as outrightly violent as possible. Shitted on the streets. Attacked strangers with broken bottles. Hit people over the head with hard objects. Kicked the guts out of people on the streets. Started fights and riots. I could barely stand being so happy. (41–42)

Janey thinks:

> Terrorism is a way to health. Health is the lusting for infin-
> ity and dying of all variants. Health is not stasis. It is not re-
> pression of lusting or dying. It is no bonds. The only desire
> of any terrorist is NO BONDS though terrorists don't desire.
> Their flaming jumping passions are infinite, but not them.
> No bonds. For these reasons terrorism and health are insepa-
> rably bound. (124)

Janey is just a child and she thinks and does truly terrible things
but she has very lovely adult thoughts and feelings so you start
to want to love her and care for her but this is exactly what her
abusers have done all her terrible life so you end up deciding
you just want her to be free which is a kind of a loss that must
be tolerated and is, frankly, what you should have wanted all
along. It makes you wonder if the point of this kind of literature
is to envelop the reader in a web of sympathetic caring, identifi-
cation with the victim, and hatred of the victimizers who come
to be everyone.

§

Janey says:

> Everyone I know lives on the roads [meaning: not in the
> *wild*]. They're creepy crawling sniveling things. I don't want
> anything to do with them. Ugh. I hate people. I can be alone.
> I can close myself up. I won't let anyone get near me. I think
> I'm off the road, but I'm dominated by fear and hatred. I'm
> as closed-up and fucked-up as everybody else. I am hell. The
> world is hell. 'No it isn't,' I scream, but I know it is. *Hell. Hell.*
> *Hell. Hell. Help. Help me. Help me. Love me.* (1978, 95, empha-
> sis added)

Hester Prynne (Hester Prynne, as in *The Scarlet Letter*) seems to be the ideal woman of the wild: "All of them even the hippies hated Hester Prynne because she was a freak and because she couldn't be anything else and because she wouldn't be quiet and hide her freakiness like a bloody Kotex and because she was wild and insane as they come" (65).

At the same time, Hester is Janey. Hester's (Janey's) husband/ father says, "I'm the guilty one [...] If I hadn't sent you alone to America, you never would have done this horrible inhuman thing" (69). For Hester, the horrible inhuman thing is getting pregnant, but for Janey it is her shame manifested as an act of *wildness*. The punishment for this wildness is worse than death. The husband/father says: "I hate you now. I don't even hate you. I just want nothing to do with you. You're not to reveal that you have ever known me or had anything to do with me. Whatever love and affection occurred between us is now dead. We're dead people" (69).

Janey ambivalently equates wildness with evil: "evil (that's the religious word for *wildness*)" (67, emphasis in original). And again, in her description of four-year-old Pearl:

> *Wild* in the Puritan New England society Hawthorne writes about means *evil anti-society criminal*. Wild. Wild. Wild [...] Pearl, according to Mr Hawthorne, wears hippie clothes and runs around in the forest and makes no distinction between what's outside her and her dreams. On the whole she doesn't make many distinctions. She doesn't know human beings exist. Sometimes she senses human beings exist. She senses a black vertical mist that's a wall pressing into her as if on top of her. She wants to scream. She feels helpless. (93)

Wildness here is something not unlike creativity in transitional space where the boundaries between self and other or self and world are fluid. The problem, according to Acker, is that transitional space and creativity are forbidden in Puritan society and ours. But maybe that is just an excuse or deflection and the problem is deeper and more internal? Janey is wild and cannot be wild because she can never be sure she is real and cannot ever truly know her needs and wants. That is why she is obsessed with sex (always: "fucking") and insists on maintaining fucking relationships in terrible conditions. It is the hope that this coupling will return her to her father.

> How do you feel about yourself when every human being you hear and see and smell every day of your being thinks you're worse than garbage […] You sense the people around you aren't right: what you did, your need, you weren't defying them to defy them, it was your need, was OK. You don't know. How can you know anything? How can you know anything? You begin to go crazy. (67–68)

§

In what can only be described as a parable about a Bear, a Beaver, and a Hideous Monster, we are immediately encouraged to note that Janey is the unwelcome Bear who yells "in a little girl's yell" (45) but at the same time worries the Monster and the Beaver when she knocks at their door. After all, says the Monster, "You might rape or kill me or you might be one of those muggers who robbed three people down the street yesterday. We know all about you" (45). Janey, of course, is both a "little girl" and a violent criminal.

Thanks to the Bear parable, we are given a clue to Janey's torment. The Bear was defeated and never got into the Monster's and the Beaver's house that he loved. In his defeat, he "has a fever he wanted to run away, but he knew if he left this bondage, there'd be nothing else left in the world" (55).

All Janey knows is bondage, as we know that her father's abusive relationship with her began earlier in her childhood and has been in many ways a lifelong experience for her. Outside of that bondage, there seemed to be nothing else, no room to grow, no way to develop appropriate feelings for herself or others and, therefore, no way to become herself outside of the context of their sexual life.

Here, we see it is her need, a child's need for help, that is the cause of a shame so profound that she cannot *know* anything. Recall that her need for help was unmet and, instead, met with rape and lasting sexual and psychological abuse. How can a child in this situation come to know herself? Her needs must be wrong because they are unmet. Others' needs matter, hers do not. Therefore, her needs must be wrong or bad. Thus, the core needs of the child's self comes to be associated with shame and loss of certainty about what she really feels or knows.

Janey and her father are still fused: "You are relief," Janey will say, "but you're in my mind: you're my characteristics again: I want relief. I want to know who you [the slave trader/Hawthorne's Reverend/her father] really are. My body aches and aches and I remember who I am" (98). Only in agony caused by another can Janey recall who she is.

Janey's dilemma is summarized neatly in the following passage. Still ostensibly describing Hester Prynne but mixing in details of Janey's own life:

> I have to figure this out: I have certain characteristics from childhood traumas, etc. Since I never had real parents… (I wasn't brought up, I just grew like a wild plant), I want love and affection the sort of love and affection you get from a parent rather than a jealous lover, and especially a father. I grew up wild, I want to stay wild. The first older man I ever fucked rejected me and his rejection put me right back into childhood desperation craziness and made me physically sick. (97)

It made her sick because it recalled her loss of her father's love, which meant the loss of her self, in spite of her attempts to be *wild*.

§

Janey has a primitive (paranoid/schizoid) understanding of love: "A couple is one who loves plus one who lets love. Couples makes up the townspeople world. If you're not part of a couple, you don't exist and no one will speak to you you outcast. Go to hell outcast" (94). Partly as a result, Janey is utterly sex-obsessed, but, pretending to be Erica Jong, Acker gets closer to Janey's true desire: "I would rather be a baby than have sex. I would rather go googoo. I would rather write: googoo. I would rather write: Fuck you up your cunts that's who I am the fuck with your money I'm not catering to you anymore [...]" (126)

To be helped like a baby is to cater to no one's needs but, rather, to be catered to. This is an experience that Janey (we must presume) has entirely missed, as her life has been centered around catering to her father's needs from an incredibly young age.

Janey's next abductor is named "Mr Linker." Mr Linker asks his slavery-recruiting gangster pupils, like a twisted Socrates, "What makes a healthy state?" (64), and the answer is: "Disease and mental instability cause health. The men who have taken the most extreme risks, who have done what may have disgusted other people or what other people would have condemned are the men who have advanced our civilization" (64).

Mr Linker's wife "had been driven crazy and then locked up for life in a New York State Sanitorium" (65). Mr Linker had been intelligent and clever but by middle age had become less so. Now, "there was no longer any chance that he could ever be intelligent, i.e., adaptable. He had become a real image, a fake" (64).

Note how what is real is false (everything is an image) and how intelligence is reduced to a kind of cleverness at adapting to what is demanded by external forces, i.e., a *false-self posture* as a kind of criminal, nihilistic philosopher. Since Janey's need to protect herself is quite strong, she attributes several evils to our "materialistic society" which "makes the universe die" and makes "everything [...] the opposite of what it really is. Good is bad. Crime is the only possible behavior" (67).

The amount of suffering Janey is willing to endure for the sake of others makes her an almost salvific figure, but ultimately a failed one. She knows her suffering has no ultimate purpose and yet she remains wedded to the idea that it will appease those who abandoned her or kicked her out. She explains to Jean Genet what she desires:

> I want you to lead me without hesitation into the land of the shadow and the monster. I want you to plunge into endless misery and hardship [...] I want you to choose evil. I want you to feel hatred and violence [...] I know where we're travelling, Genet, and I know why we're travelling there. It's not just to travel, but it's so those others who kicked me out have a chance of being at peace, have a chance of knowing the land of the monster without going there. (139)

While in captivity with the Persian slave trader, Janey's lyrical poem of joy and madness abruptly changes to her "slave poem" which begins:

> Why am I existing?
> Just to be a slave?
> List of my slave duties:
>
> (1) Body slavery: I have to eat and get shelter so need money. Also my body likes sex and rich food and I'll do anything for these.
>
> (2) Mind slavery: I want more than just money. I live in a partially human world and I want people to think and feel certain ways about me. So I try to set up certain networks, mental-physical, in time and space to get what I want. (I also set up these networks to get money.) These networks become history and culture (if they work) and as such, turn against me and take away time and space. They tell me what to do.

The world I perceive, everything I perceive are indicators of my boring needs, Otherwise there's nothing. I might as well not exist.

I don't think I care about anything. All my emotions, no matter how passionate, are based on my needs. (111)

Janey's and Acker's argument here is that we are all slaves, whether literal or figurative, if we want anything. Wants (like needs) are the real danger because, in setting up "networks" to obtain help, one is forced to become other than who one is. They "turn against" Janey and "tell [her] what to do." What is more, needs and wants are only believed to be fulfillable in exchange (or bargain) for something valuable about the self: in this case, the self's autonomy, since once one permits one's wants to control one's behavior ("What else can one do?" Janey might ask), one ends up being controlled by the networks and institutions set up to achieve those initial ends.

§

All of this is understood to be inevitable. Indeed, "loving everything and rolling in it like it's all gooky shit" is Janey's expression for *not growing up*. She continues: "goddamnit make a living grow up no you don't want to do that" (67). The "gooky shit" is

black fur on top of skin ice-cold water iron crinkly leaves seeing three brown branches against branches full of leaves against dark green leaves through this the misty grey wanders in garbage on the streets up to your knees and unshaven men lying under cocaine piled on top of cocaine colours colours everything happening! one thing after another thing! (67)

Apparently, this is what you love when you "hate and despise and detest yourself 'cause you've been in prison so long. It's possible to get angrier and angrier" (66).

Once Janey is released from her prison and permitted to sell herself on the streets, Janie discovers that she has cancer, which is "the outward condition of the condition of being screwed-up" (123). Now, all she feels she can do is die:

> Janey was learning to love herself. Everything was shooting out of her body like an orgasming volcano. All the pain and misery she had been feeling, crime and terror on the streets had come out. She was no longer totally impotent and passive about her lousy situation. Now she could do something about the pain the world: she could die. (116)

Imprisoned again but this time in in Alexandria, Janey sits in a cell as judges walk by to "tell[] her who she is." Judge 2 says: "You whine and snivel. You don't stand up for yourself. You act like you do totally to please other people. You're a piece of shit. You're not real" (133).

"All she does is weep… You should get rid of her. We might be animals, but at least we know how to keep our feelings locked in us. Women are worse than animals" (132). Janey had not discovered a way to be wild; only a way to passively accept her fate.

This makes one think of Bresson's famous film, *Au Hazard Balthazar,* where the tortured being is a donkey, as opaque and passive as can be, as he is abused over and over again throughout his life. All of this is presented of course without any emotion, as is typical of Bresson's work.

Janey asks a Rebel, after escaping from "gaol" with Jean Genet: "Please tell me if the world is horrible and if my life is horrible and if there's no use in trying to change, or if there is anything else. Is desire OK?" (138). Is desire OK? Is *my* desire OK? One suspects that her desire is not OK with her and that, what is worse, she may not know her own desire at all.

If she finds it, it will be destructive and would need considerable help, over a long period of time, to begin to modify Janey's internal world. This help would entail replacing the objects in Janey's inner world with benign ones, so that her attempts to fulfill her desires need not be "criminal" or involve so much aggression.

In any case, this fundamental question about desire and fulfilling internal needs haunts Janey to the end. Janey dies without embellishment by Acker. Later, "many other Janeys were born and these Janeys covered the earth" (165).

II.

It sometimes seems that a malignant fate pursues [certain] men and women [...] The persons themselves apparently do not do anything to bring about their destiny. What happens — and it is always the same — happens to them; it just seems to occur whatever they do or omit doing. Since these individuals show no obvious neurotic symptoms, some psychiatrists have spoken of a "neurosis of destiny" in similar cases. — Theodor Reik

The Painted Bird (1976) by Jerzy Kosiński begins with a description of the situation of an unnamed six-year-old boy who is left to the care of Eastern European (Polish) villagers as World War II threatened their unnamed city in 1939. In spite of the historical references and the frequent grim depictions of concentration camps, we may read the story as an allegorical search for help that ends in a combination of dejection and autonomy.

Like Acker's *Blood and Guts in High School,* it is non-stop atrocity torture lit. The boy–narrator is either alone in fear or being brutally victimized. He runs, or is chased, from village to village, under the direst possible circumstances and, no matter where he goes, he finds himself utterly "without human help" (Kosiński 1976, 28).

The desolate scenery, the poverty and poor living conditions, the rampant violence, lust, and destruction all leave the boy in a world that is godforsaken. In a time of plague:

Children gazed tearfully at the blue-spotted faces of their dead parents. The plague persisted. The villagers would come to the thresholds of their huts, raise their eyes from the earthly dust, and search for God. He alone could assuage their bitter sorrow. He alone could bestow the mercy of serene sleep on these tormented human bodies. He alone could change the horrible enigmas of the disease into ageless health. He alone could deaden the pain of a mother mourning for her lost child. But God, in His impenetrable wisdom, waited. (22)

After his first caretaker, Marta, dies and her hut burns to the ground, the boy ends up in a ravine and begins to think of his parents, much in the same way that he thinks about God:

Everything around was silent. I believed that now I would meet my parents in the ravine. I believed that, even far away, they must know all that had happened to me. Wasn't I their child? What were parents for if not to be with their children in times of danger? (14)

His parents having abandoned him "without human help," the boy is left in a world whose inhabitants are vicious and often compared to animals. As a miller's wife and a plowboy fantasize about making love, a tomcat and a tabby cat in heat struggle in the corner. "Stupid Ludmila," before she is killed, is a free, "strange colored bird flying to faraway worlds" (49), just as Lekh, her lover, cruelly paints birds' wings and bodies before returning them to their nests, so that they are attacked and killed as outsiders and intruders by their kin.

When a boy was thrown from a passing railcar heading to a nearby concentration camp to save his life, the villagers hosting the boy found him half-dead and stripped him of his shoes and clothes:

I tried to think what he had thought before dying. When he was tossed out of the train his parents or his friends no doubt assured him that he would find *human help* which would save him from a horrible death in the great furnace. He probably felt cheated, deceived. He would have preferred to cling to the warm bodies of his father and mother in the packed car, to feel the pressure and smell the hot tart odors, the presence of other people, knowing that he was not alone […]. (99, emphasis added)

§

The boy goes through several stages in his attempt to figure out life's meaning and, in the end, we are unsure where he has settled. The goal, in any case, in figuring out meaning in the world, is to determine the best way to get help and to improve one's life. Meaning is not sought for its own sake, but because the world around one has become insane.

At first, the boy describes the extraordinary beauty and perfection of an ss officer, then, as the officer inspects him, he feels a terrible shame mixed with awe:

I felt like a squashed caterpillar oozing in the dust, a creature that could not harm anyone yet aroused loathing and disgust. In the presence of his [the ss officer's] resplendent being, armed in all the symbols of might and majesty, I was genuinely ashamed of my appearance. I had nothing against his killing me […] I knew my fate was being decided in some manner, but it was matter of indifference to me. I placed infinite confidence in the decision of the man facing me. I knew that he possessed powers unattainable by ordinary people. (114)

Soon, he turns to Christian prayer for support, having learned that certain prayers earn a person a specific number of "days of indulgence" (126–32). This is the boy's way of deciphering his experience, his regular beatings, maulings, and humiliations, and he is quick to reproach himself for not having thought of prayers and indulgences before.

But after he is made a stand-in acolyte and drops the missal from the altar, he is thrown into a deep latrine trench, from which he barely emerges alive. When he does, his voice is gone (138–41). He reflects:

There must have been some cause for the loss of my speech. Some greater force, with which I had not yet managed to communicate, commanded my destiny. I began to doubt that it could be God or one of his saints. With my credit secured by vast numbers of prayers, my days of indulgence must have been innumerable; God had no reason to inflict such terrible punishment on me. (141)

Yet, as he falls in love with a sexually abusive, older woman named Ewka, he returns to a very different understanding of himself, now as an aggressor.

I forgot my fate of a Gypsy mute destined for fire. I ceased to be a goblin jeered at by herders, casting spells on children and animals. In my dreams I turned into a tall, handsome man, fair-skinned, blue-eyed, with hair like pale autumn leaves. I became a German officer in a tight, black uniform. Or I turned into a birdcatcher, familiar with all the secret paths of the woods and marshes. (147)

Needless to say, there is a powerful theme of what Anna Freud would call "identification with the aggressor" in the book. But here, identification with the aggressor and with various groups are survival-mechanisms for the boy. They respond to his dream of receiving ample "human help." When he sees Ewka having sex with a goat at the prodding of her own father,

something collapsed inside me. My thoughts fell apart and shattered into broken fragments like a smashed jug [...] All these events became suddenly clear and obvious. They explained the expression I had often heard people use about people who were very successful in life: "He is in league with the Devil." Peasants also accused one another of accepting help from various demons, such as Lucifer, Cadaver, Mammon, Exterminator, and many others. (151)

Remark his emphasis on help. "Evil Ones" are favored in life and their "malignant seed" offered those worthy

all the help which might be needed. [...] From the moment of signing a pact with the Devil, the more harm, misery, injury, and bitterness a man could inflict around him, the more help he could expect. [...] Only those with a sufficiently powerful passion for hatred, greed, revenge, or torture to obtain some objective seemed to make a good bargain with the powers of Evil. Others, confused, uncertain of their aim, lost between curses and prayers [...] struggled through life alone, without help from either God or the Devil. (152)

Later, the boy reconceptualizes his world yet again, this time by watching the example of the Kalmuks (Soviet deserters whom the German Army permitted to scourge and pillage villages beyond the front), who are also black-haired and black-eyed. But here, in witnessing their extraordinary violence, he feels hopeless: "There could be no mercy for such as me [...] in common with this horde of savages" (178–79).

When he meets Gavrila and Mitka of an occupying Soviet regiment, he finds yet another system of meaning in which there is no God, only people whose actions take on collective importance (187–89). Now the Soviet soldiers take over for the tall, German solider as the ego-ideal, as the boy begins to recognize the difference between what the Germans and the Soviets were doing. Now the boy is lightly buoyed by Gavrila's stance: "In this world there were realistic ways of promoting goodness, and there were people who had dedicated their whole lives to it" (191).

Yet, when he is eventually transferred to an orphanage, he refuses to speak his native language and tells the staff that he is

Russian (211). When he is eventually reunited with his parents, he is less than pleased:

> I knew that rejoining my parents meant the end of all my dreams of becoming a great inventor of fuses for changing people's color, of working in the land of Gavrila and Mitka, where today was already tomorrow. My world was becoming cramped like the attic of a peasant's shed. At all times a man risked falling into the snares of those who hated and wanted to persecute him, or into the arms of those who loved and wished to protect him. (226)

These two options are treated as if they were the same, because "I could not readily accept the idea of suddenly becoming someone's real son, of being caressed and cared for [...] smothered by their love and protection" (226–28). In fact, he feels like one of Lekh's painted birds at this moment, "which some unknown force was pulling [him] toward his kind" (227).

Near the end, the boy begins to go out only at night, to take to serious crime with his friend, the Silent One (216), and to the "night city," for "in daytime the world was at peace. The war continued at night" (232). In a moment of anger, he breaks his younger step-brother's arm and is eventually sent to a ski instructor's home in the mountains, where a blizzard eventually lands him in the hospital.

Finally, it would seem that he has forsaken all of his idols in an attempt to make sense of the world on his own, albeit in a bitter and unhappy way: "Every one of us stood alone, and the sooner a man realizes that all the Gavrilas, Mitkas, and Silent Ones were expendable, the better for him. It mattered little if one was mute; people did not understand one another anyway" (233). He soon receives a phone call from an unidentified caller and, miraculously, his speech returns

Sisyphus Doesn't Want Your Help

Sisyphus herded cattle. Beyond that, he was a cheat and a liar. Near him, on Corinth, lived Autolycus, who was a master thief whom Sisyphus suspected of stealing. Therefore, one day Sisyphus engraved all of his cattle's hooves "with the monogram 'ss' or, some say, with the words 'Stolen by Autolycus'" (Graves 1955, 216). After proving Autolycus's theft, Sisyphus snuck into Autolycus's house and seduced his daughter, Anticleia (a woman at first literally "without fame"), who would later give birth to Odysseus, whose renowned cunning has been attributed to his father's manner of seduction.[1]

According to Robert Graves, although Sisyphus "promoted Corinthian commerce," "his contemporaries knew him as the worst kind of knave on earth," presumably because of his extramarital activities (216). Legend has it that Sisyphus, enraged that

---

1   Odysseus's nickname, "Hypsipylon," is the masculine form of Hypsipyle, the title of a play by Euripides and a legendary woman who saved her father when the women of Lemnos murdered all the men on the island for adultery (after Aphrodite made all the women smell so bad that their husbands took up with Thracian women imported to the island). When the other women learned that she had spared her father, out of vengeance she was sold into slavery to Lycurgus, king of Nemea. There, while she was acting as nurse to Opheltes, the king's infant son, she became distracted (ostensibly by the needs of the Seven Against Thebes) and, in her neglect, the child was killed by a snake (see Edwards 2002; k-web 2018).

Salmoneus had usurped the Thessalian crown, was told by the Oracle at Delphi to sire children with his nieces, which he did. But after learning his true motive was not love, Sisyphus's niece Tyro killed the two sons she had borne him. Sisyphus then entered the marketplace holding the dead bodies and falsely accused Salmoneus of incest and murder, exiling him (217).

Sisyphus knew that Aegina had been abducted by Zeus and carried off to Oenone, later called simply Aegina, but he refused to tell Aegina's father, the River-God Asopus, what he knew until Asopus gave Corinth a perpetual spring. When Sisyphus finally told Asopus what he knew, Zeus punished him for telling "divine secrets" to Asopus, and summoned Hades, who had enough trouble capturing Sisyphus, for even Hades was handcuffed by trickery and was kept in Sisyphus's house for several days (217).

After Ares resolved the situation, Sisyphus once again implemented a ruse to keep him out of the underworld. Before descending to Tartarus, Sisyphus told his wife Merope not to bury him. Knowing that Persephone would have sympathy for this situation, Sisyphus went to Persephone and argued that he should be left on the far side of the river Styx. He begged: "Let me return to the upper world, arrange for my burial, and avenge the neglect shown me. My presence here is most irregular. I will be back within three days" (218). But "as soon as he found himself once again under the light of the sun" (218), he reneged on his promise and remained in the upper world.[2]

Sisyphus is sometimes spelled Sesephus and may be the Greek variant of Tesup, the Hittite Sun-God. And, as the one who was originally injured by Autolycus's theft, Sisyphus recalls

---

2 It is hard not to notice the relationship here between help and betrayal. Help is used as an excuse for injustice and crime; help is offered by some and denied by others, both Gods and people. This relationship is not unique to the myth of Sisyphus. One might even say it runs throughout Greek mythology like a leitmotif of paranoia. The meaning of this has much to do with an ancient ideal of the hero as someone who neither gives nor receives (nor needs) help.

the story of Jacob and Laban in *Genesis,* in which Rachel steals "household gods" from her father, his uncle (219n1).

§

At this moment, Albert Camus (1991b) enters into the legend and, to a great degree, makes it his own. Camus and other scholars disagree and, eventually, demur on the reason that Sisyphus is given such a memorable and extraordinary punishment, but Camus makes Sisyphus into a Promethean figure by claiming that he risked his fate with the gods for the sake of water for his countrymen: "To the celestial thunderbolts he preferred the benediction of water" (119).

Sisyphus is given a "shameless stone" (Graves 1955, 218–19), originally a Corinthian sun-disk, and is ordered to push the stone/disk to the top of a steep hill at the top of which stood the vault of Heaven (219, n. 2). Of course, Sisyphus can never complete his task. Each time he gets close to the top, the stone rolls back down by its own weight, Sisyphus returns to the base of the hill to retrieve it, and he begins again, "though sweat bathes his limbs, and a cloud of dust rises above his head" (218).

At some point, Sisyphus, the trickster and rebel, is broken. He apparently no longer wishes to escape Hades, nor longs for the light of day, but fully accepts his punishment. According to Camus, he is not *an* but *the* "absurd hero [...] as much through his passions as through his torture" (1991b, 120). But neither his passions nor his acceptance of his torture seem particularly heroic. According to Camus, Sisyphus's "scorn of the gods, his hatred of death, and his passion for life won him that unspeakable penalty in which the whole being is exerted toward accomplishing nothing. This is the price that must be paid for the passions of this earth" (120).

Camus claims that at the very moments when Sisyphus walks down the hill to retrieve his stone, having failed to reach the vault of Heaven yet again, that he is most "conscious." It is also the moment when he becomes "superior to his fate" and "stronger than his rock" (121). Sisyphus, claims Camus, is superior to his fate and stronger than his rock because Sisyphus knows that, no matter his labors, the stone will roll back down the hill and he will, once again, fail at his task. Sisyphus "knows the whole extent of his wretched condition: it is what he thinks of during his descent" (121), unlike the "workman of today" who, without the same (Marxist?) "consciousness," believes each day that his labors will lead him somewhere new.

But the story gets stranger. The myth, according to Camus, becomes tragic only "at the rare moments when it becomes conscious" (121). We may forgive Camus's mix-up here, lest we understand him to mean that the story, itself, becomes conscious of itself. Rather, what he means is that Sisyphus, "powerless and rebellious," now "crowns his victory" by dint of "the same lucidity that was to constitute his torture" (121).

For Camus, at least in his early writings such as *The Myth of Sisyphus,* we may say that lucid sacrifice is better than unconscious contentment. Why? Only if tragic and lucid sacrifice represented an act of rebellion, not so much against a real ill of this world as against fate, "the world" itself, or the gods.

But why are rebellion and victory so important? The unfortunate answer is that "there is no fate that cannot be surmounted by scorn" (121). Scorn, or contempt, at the gods does little to help improve Sisyphus's or anyone else's condition; indeed, it does the opposite. Sisyphus consciously conforms to the requirements of his eternal punishment and it is this conscious conformity that Camus valorizes, so long as it is mixed with *hatred.*

It is as if Sisyphus were saying with his actions, "I accept this torture for the crimes of passion I have committed, for which I do not repent," like Oedipus, in a moment of clarity, who cries out, "Despite so many ordeals, my advanced age and the nobility of my soul make me conclude that all is well," which, for Camus, is "the recipe for absurd victory," as "ancient wisdom confirms modern heroism" (122).

§

Let us consider this matter further. Sisyphus asks for help several times in his life, even from Persephone, who grants him a temporary return to the world of the living. For his crimes, however, Sisyphus is condemned to the realm of the dead. Nothing around him is alive or vibrant. And yet, according to Camus, he may descend "in joy" just as easily as "in sorrow" (121). To be joyful, then, is to scorn or spit in the face of one's victimizers, to "drive[] out of this world a god who had come into it with […] a preference for futile sufferings. [Now] it makes of fate a human matter, which must be settled among men. All Sisyphus' joy is contained therein. His fate belongs to him. His rock is his thing. Likewise, the absurd man, when he contemplates his torment, silences all the idols" (122–23).

We find a temptation here to make suffering into a masochistic ideal. Camus seems to be saying that as long as one is conscious of one's pain, as long as "fate" becomes a human matter and not a metaphysical or religious one, then one can claim victory over it because one's consciousness is, in itself, an act of revolt.

There is something sloppy about the psychology of the argument here. It borders on magical thinking or what Hanna Segal would call a "symbolic equation," where symbols are mistaken for the things themselves. Indeed, Germaine Brée asks: "What is a revolt that ends in the acceptance of a Sisyphus?" (1964, 208). Is becoming conscious so *acquisitive* that it means not just being aware of, but *possessing* all of one's circumstances? And even so, if one's circumstances are bleak, why is this a victory unless the battle is a battle between unconscious suffering and conscious suffering?

For Camus, life *is* a battle between unconscious suffering and conscious suffering. The problem is that this vision of victory still leaves us in a desolate and helpless world: "In the universe suddenly restored to its silence, the myriad wondering little voices of the earth rise up. Unconscious, secret calls, invitations

83

from all the faces, they are the necessary reverse and price of victory" (1991b, 123).

Do we no longer hear the voices of others in absurd victory? Or do we hear them but ignore them because we know that, for them, there is no succor. "The absurd man says yes and his effort will henceforth be unceasing. If there is a personal fate, there is no higher destiny, or at least there is but one which he concludes is inevitable and despicable" (123). Having accepted that his destiny is both inevitable and despicable, the absurd person is "a blind man eager to see who knows that the night has no end" (123), which makes of him something of a fool.

The blind man needs help to see, but Camus refuses and insists, instead, not only that he does not need help, but that it is the seeing man who needs help to see the endless night that the blind man perceives. The real, unconscious goal here is *to share the darkness* with others, with all others, until the entire universe is "divested of illusions and lights" (6).

We always find a way. We always find a way to give ourselves up. To give ourselves Over. Over and over. To give ourselves to something or someone. Even to gods imagined by orphans.

Camus believes that he inhabits a "condition in which I can have peace only by refusing to know and to live, in which the appetite for conquest bumps into walls that defy its assaults [...]. Everything is ordered in such a way as to bring into being that poisoned peace produced by thoughtlessness, lack of heart, or fatal renunciations" (20). These conditions are, for Camus, certainties to which "I must sacrifice everything [...] to be able to maintain them," and even "adapt my behavior to them" (21).

In the end, Camus claims that Sisyphus finds contentment by struggling toward the summit, which is why he famously proclaims, "one must imagine Sisyphus happy [*il faut imaginer Sisyphe heureux*]" (123). But, as Brée points out, we are forced to ask ourselves: what summit? "The ethics peculiar to Camus's four preceding heroes are derived from the assertion that there is no 'upward' path. But Sisyphus is now a moral hero, a stoic, convinced that, in spite of the gods, man's dignity requires him to 'struggle toward the summit'" (1964, 208).

Camus is arguing that, rather than reconciling it, wishing it away, or fighting it, we must accept and adapt to the truth we know about our lives: that *we do not matter* in an unhelpful and unreasonable world. We are impotent to change our plight, but Camus offers us what Jean-Paul Sartre would call an invitation to *mauvaise foi* (bad faith) if we can accept absurdity as a "given" and act accordingly.

Camus has worked hard to argue that rational and spiritual perfection are impossible, and that human activities are not meaningful, that all that eventually holds truth for Camus is absurdity, the "confrontation of this irrational [world] and the wild longing for clarity whose call echoes in the human heart" (1991b, 21). Is this call echoing in the human heart an example of "the myriad wondering little voices of the earth [...] unconscious, secret calls, invitations from all the faces," which are "the necessary reverse and price of victory" (123)? If so, we must ignore them and make sacrifices to this absurd confrontation and to the conclusions to which it leads until, eventually, we must even adapt our behavior to suit what appears to be an impossible set of demands. After all, if one refuses to take leaps of faith or to commit "philosophical suicide," one is left with a "ravaged world in which the impossibility of knowledge is established, in which everlasting nothingness seems the only reality and irremediable despair seems the only attitude" (25).

For Camus, holding onto brokenness is a sign of our wholeness, because we have not given in to the desire to forget, to ignore, or to cheat the logic of absurdity. The key is finding out what is broken. It is the early loss of help and togetherness that breaks the child's world. In the face of disruption or damage to early relationships, one has to contend with "the contradictory desires at once to search for and recover the lost relationship and to escape from painful reminders of loss" (Marris 1986, vii). This search and the resulting code of "absurd ethics" serves both purposes well.

§

This is how we make meaning: Family relationships organize our purposes and attachments, which are filtered through an interpretive context or structure of meaning to organize our actions,

> for the ability to learn from experience relies on the stability of the interpretations by which we predict the pattern of events. We assimilate new experiences by placing them in the context of a familiar, reliable construction of reality. This structure in turn rests not only on the regularity of events themselves, but on the continuity of their meaning. [...] Confidence in the predictability of our surroundings rests not only on the accident of living [...] in a consistent world, but on our ability to abstract from particular events the underlying laws which govern them, in ways which are relevant to our human purposes. (Marris 1986, 6)

But, of course, this regularity and predictability are precisely what Camus seems to have lost in *The Myth of Sisyphus,* where there is "a direct connection between this feeling [of absurdity] and the longing for death" (1991b, 6), which is the very subject of Camus's essay: "This divorce between man and his life, the actor and his setting is properly the feeling of absurdity" (6).

> The social order evolves from the physical order, as we perceive it. But the principle which determines the predictability of the social environment are even more obviously of our own making than the sense we impose [or fail to impose] on the natural world. [...] Each symbolic grammar is a language to express the meaning of relationships — their purposes, expected patterns of interaction, the framework of assumptions about the world into which they fit. Any challenge to it is likely at first to provoke *bewildered resentment.* (Marris 1986, 7, emphasis added)

Remember, it is not the falsity of the system of meanings that generates the absurd dilemma, but rather a disruption in any system of meaning. Even Camus agrees that "a world that can be explained even with bad reasons is a familiar world" (1991b, 6). Nonetheless, "what we cannot do is survive without a system of some kind for predicting the course of events. It does not matter that the system may be false on another system's terms, so long as it identifies experiences in a way which enables people to attach meaning to them and respond" (Marris 1986, 6).

The system holds to the extent that it provides help in a regular and predictable way. Indeed, "the predictability of behaviour is profoundly important, and it depends not only on some shared sense of the meaning of relationships but on conventions of expressing this meaning, which must be insisted upon all the more anxiously because it is arbitrary" (7).

Camus takes the destruction of meaning to mean that no system of purposes and attachments can function for him or others when it is, shall we say, *his* world that has collapsed, not necessarily *ours*. Or, it is ours if we share in or identify with his particular dilemma, which is being helpless. In this way, helplessness is the new idol to which we sacrifice ourselves.

> I judge the notion of the absurd to be essential and consider that it can stand as the first of my truths. [...] If I judge that a thing is true, I must preserve it. [...] For me, the sole datum is the absurd. The first and, after all, the only condition of my inquiry is to preserve the very thing that crushes me, consequently to respect what I consider essential in it. [...] A man who has become conscious of the absurd is forever bound to it. A man devoid of hope and conscious of being so has ceased to belong to the future. That is natural. (Camus 1991b, 31)

Absurdity has made its way into "essentials," "truth," and even "nature," which must be preserved, whereas, earlier, such notions and such behavior were treated as highly suspect.

Camus is quick to point out that absurdity must lie not in the world or in the self but in the relation between the two. But he is not so circumspect about the construct of meaning itself. That is, Camus seems to expect meaning to *reside in* the world and, what is more, that the world should present this meaning to him when he needs it. At this point, the idea of human meaning becomes nonsense as it would be *given* and, to the extent that it is unchanging and unchangeable, inhuman.

§

Camus's vision of the human being was, of course, that of a noble but tragic creature inhabiting a tragic (absurd) universe. In the first essay of *The Myth of Sisyphus,* Camus refers to either "the absurd" or "absurdity" as a deprivation of "the memory of a lost home or the hope of a promised land" (6), a "divorce between man and his life" (6), an "odd state of soul in which the void becomes eloquent" (12), a moment when "the stage sets collapse" (12), "the denseness and strangeness of the world" (14), "the familiar and yet alarming brother we encounter in our own photograph" (15), "the elementary and definitive aspect of the [mortal] adventure" (15), and "the confrontation between the human need and the unreasonable silence of the world" (28). Here we find an intellectual universe in which the essential realities of objects and forces such as "the world," "the void," and "the soul," are more or less taken for granted, and, in that sense, are not terribly helpful.

The final definition cited in the paragraph above, however, does advance our purpose, for when it is combined with Camus's later elaboration of absurdity as the conflict or "divorce between the mind that desires and the world that disappoints" (50), we are able to understand Camus's vision of absurdity as a flaw or incongruity or lack (or *manque,* in Lacanian language) *within a relationship*. Camus contended that if there is absurdity in the human condition it is not simply an emanation of the human being nor of "the world," but of the relationship between the two, specifically of "the confrontation between the human need [*l'appel humain*] and the unreasonable silence of the world" (28).

This phrase — *l'appel humain* — is pregnant with meaning inasmuch as the notion of a person or child calling out for help or succor, but finding no reply, brings to mind the deprived or abandoned child faced with the psychically annihilating silence of a missing or depriving caregiver. It is unfortunate that Justin O'Brien's (confounding) translation of the French word *appel* as "need" has for so many years obscured this obvious resonance and imagery. An *appel* is, first and foremost, a call or cry. In a second sense, it is an appeal.

Thus, what is absurd, for Camus, is that the human call, the human cry, the human appeal for help, is met with silence. Absurdity is "born" — Camus's use of the verb *naître* also calls to mind childbirth, infancy, and childhood — in the chasm between an expectant cry and a terrifying absence, much as the subjective existence of the child is threatened with destruction if cries for the parent are unheeded.

When the word *appel* is encountered again in *The Myth of Sisyphus,* Camus argues that the project of the absurd person is to find out if it is possible to live *sans appel,* "without appeal" (53). In this case, Camus uses *appel* to play on the juridical meaning of "appealing" to a higher authority, and Camus seems to say: If the absurd person cries out expectantly but finds that the object of his need is silent, absent, or even radically diminished, then declaring this experience to be "absurd" entails the refusal to make any further appeals. This indignant refusal, which rings of Aesop's "sour grapes," seems necessary for Camus if we are to maintain our dignity, or, at least, if we are to protect ourselves from further disappointment.

Camus, then, asks us to preserve our awareness of absurdity, of the disharmony between our expectations and the realities of silence, loss, abandonment, and deprivation we face. To refuse to "appeal" them, in one sense, is a kind of appeal, since we are exhorted to "[keep] the absurd alive" by "contemplating it" (54), "through constant awareness, ever revived, ever alert" to hold such agonies before our minds in order to "preserve the very thing that crushes [us]" (31).

Even if it were possible to *contemplate* absurdity without losing ourselves in an imagination decoupled from reality, why would we wish to preserve the very thing that crushes us? Why is "the important thing [...] not to be cured, but to live with one's ailments" (38)? One answer is that when we declare conditions or events to be absurd, we paradoxically refuse to call (appeal) them *and* call (*appel*) them back, *binding* ourselves to their absence or deficiency by refusing to mourn their loss. Indeed, even Camus knows that absurdity "binds [the mind that desires and the world that disappoints] one to the other as only hatred can weld two creatures together" (21; 50).

For Camus, this binding hatred is built into the natures both of the human being and of the world. But, in psychoanalytic terms, one might say of such a perspective that it denies the possibility that what makes human existence absurd is a product of the human psyche: that we make experience absurd or not absurd. Put another way, Camus's universe — his ontology, if you will — consists of reified supra-human objects and forces that operate independently of the psyche and that actively contribute to the absurdity of the human experience: such as "the world," "the void," and "the soul," and so on.

When he wrote, he wrote of common men. As if to re-create them left a word unspoken, and utterly unique to him, in his soul. He never wrote of the soul. He saw the thoughtless men along the street and wrote: These men imagine divides unto which they unbecome, between themselves. They live within them. They are, themselves, a mess of divides imagined: inside / outside / real / imagined / Heaven / Earth. These are enjoined profoundly to their wrinkled overcoats, wrinkled cigarettes, wrinkled faces, which, too, are adequate to delineate the men I see as in need of help, having understood nothing, sought for nothing, sacrificed themselves for nothing, for there, for them, is nothing. *He wished to make the words appear on the thoughtless men's*

*mouths. The words to him were painful yet delight. He intuited
the robustness of the soul. He never wrote of the soul.*

Confronted with such material, a psychoanalyst would likely
note an unwillingness or failure to "own" the emotions that constitute the absurd feeling or experience. That is, to the extent
that we locate responsibility for absurdity in objects and forces
outside of ourselves — and while Camus places partial responsibility on our shoulders, more often he gives the impression that
it is really "the world" that denies us, that it is the world that is
primarily responsible for our absurd condition — we impover-
ish ourselves as agents or subjects who define and determine
our own experience.

Camus's "external" objects — of which perhaps the most important and yet the least well-defined is "the world" — are what a
thoughtful psychoanalyst might understand as externalizations
of internal objects created in the process of sorting out (or failing to sort out) internal dilemmas, particularly those associated
with abandonment and helplessness.[3]

---

3   It would, of course, be foolish to be too strict or binary in our approach
     to the "inner" and "outer" worlds, as these worlds overlap to a significant
     degree, and this overlap is part of the foundation of the school of psychoa-
     nalysis to which I will turn most frequently in this essay, the school of
     object-relations theory, which contends that our inner world is shaped by
     our interactions and relationships with objects (others) and that internal
     models and internal objects are created and then managed, repressed, or,
     quite frequently, cast out into the world to be re-enacted throughout life.
     Externalization, a crucial part of the psychic economy that must rid the
     inner world of objects that are too dangerous or toxic to contain, is used,
     therefore, when managing internal conflicts or dilemmas proves to be
     impossible. External objects are "created" and imbued with qualities (or
     the absence of qualities, i.e., depriving or withholding natures) to contain
     what cannot be contained within the self.

§

One problem with raging against externalized objects is that these objects are created and shaped almost exclusively by fantasy, by the mind of the one who rejects them. Thus, hatred of an abandoning object or envy of the privileged person who do not seem to experience the same abandonment translates into a form of hatred and self-hatred. The position of one who rages against the impossibility of being "at home" in the world — a position embodied not only in Camus's "absurd stance" but in much late modern and postmodern thought (see Bowker 2014) — comes to resemble the position of the melancholic who finds himself stuck in a "mental constellation of [perpetual] revolt" (Freud 1957, 248).

At times, Camus's project seems more or less in line with the "normal" work of mourning Freud described in his famous essay, "Mourning and Melancholia," in which reality-testing helps the individual to see "that the loved object no longer exists, and [to proceed] to demand that all libido should be withdrawn from its attachments to that object" (244). As opposed to the process of mourning, in melancholia the assimilation of loss and the prospect of creating attachments to new objects are rejected. The loss itself is left unmourned, and even remains unconscious to the melancholy person, who nevertheless rages violently against it and against himself.

As Freud famously put it, when "the shadow of the [lost] object [falls] upon the ego" (249), the abandoned self punishes itself along with the bad object-in-self to which it is now bound by both love and hatred, finding pleasure in identifying with the pain-inducing qualities of the object, which is to say, in inflicting pain and suffering on the self.

> If the love for the object [...] takes refuge in narcissistic identification, then the hate comes into operation on this substitutive object, abusing it, debasing it, making it suffer and deriving sadistic satisfaction from its suffering. The self-tormenting in melancholia, which is without a doubt enjoy-

able, signifies [...] a satisfaction of trends of sadism and hate which relate to an object, and which have been turned round upon the subject's own self. (251)

For Freud, both mourning and melancholia may be occasioned not only by the loss of a loved person, but by "the loss of some abstraction which has taken the place of one, such as one's country, liberty, [or] an ideal" (243). Thus, losses, abuses, tragedies, and traumas of all varieties, large and small, individual and collective, may generate our need to mourn or to become melancholy, to either adjust to loss or to revolt against it. Because the losses for which Camus recommends the absurd stance are often of a broader, more political order, we may understand absurdity as a psychological posture of perpetual, melancholic revolt.

Lately, melancholic revolt has been valorized as something heroic, along lines quite similar to those advanced by Camus. For Jacques Derrida, for instance, the failure or impossibility of mourning is rooted in an ethical injunction not to erase the other. Derrida argues that mourning *should* fail because, when it fails, it succeeds in leaving the other intact. It is "a tender rejection, a movement of renunciation, which leaves the other alone, outside, over there, in his death, outside of us" (1989, 35). In her essay on Levinas and Kristeva, Ewa Ziarek draws out the logical conclusion to Derrida's argument by claiming that the melancholic's inability to heal from grief must be recognized as a valiant refusal, undertaken with "unusual sobriety," resulting in "a powerful critique of the desire to master alterity through the order of representation" (1993, 73).

But these accounts get the idea of separateness wrong. To refuse to complete mourning, to refuse to (re-)cognize the lost friend, is actually to refuse to let go of the lost friend. To reject our interiorizations and imaginations of the person (see Derrida 2001) does not leave the other alone or "intact," but seeks to preserve, without (re-)cognizing, the friend's vital uniqueness. In successful mourning, we are able to admit that this vital uniqueness has been lost and cannot be preserved because the living person is gone. To (re-)cognize and mourn a loss is to permit the self to separate from the lost and cared-for object, and to permit the object to separate from the self.

Refusals of mourning, then, are refusals of the possibility of thinking about and relating to a lost beloved object, even an object that exists now only in memory or fantasy. They are refusals of communication between self and object in favor of a permanent (although agonizing) *binding* or communion. Members of a family or group who can only find connection through proximity, sameness, and belonging commune in melancholia and even in hatred, because communication is impossible (see Bowker 2016, 63–77). In Julia Kristeva's words, they "nostalgically fall back on the real object (the Thing) of their loss, which is just what they do not manage to lose, to which they remain painfully riveted" (1989, 43–44).

The absurd posture, then, seems to be motivated by a refusal to mourn loss, to understand it, and to "appeal" it, all of which seems to afford the absurd self some protection against experiencing the most devastating effects of loss. Instead, a specious freedom and innocence are asserted as the absurd person attempts to "establish [their] lucidity in the midst of what negates it [...] [and to] exalt man before what crushes him" (Camus 1991b, 87–88).

In a similar way, survivors traumatized by the horrific violence of the Nazi Holocaust have been noted to resist psychological healing on the grounds that such healing is too similar to "granting Hitler a posthumous victory. [...] To them, self-integration appears antithetical to the only justification of their survival — that they are obligated to be angry witnesses against the outrage of the Holocaust" (Krystal 1995, 83).

Instead, "scorn," for the self's aspirations to healing, meaning, and being alive is the tool of the absurd rebel (Camus 1991b, 121). Scorn prevents the absurd rebel from making meaning from loss. However, scorn also affords the rebel, by a circuitous route, a way to reconnect with something involved in the lost object-relationship, something whose loss would be intolerable. This loss is the loss of righteous indignation, a combination of assumed innocence and rage, that may overtake the character of the absurd rebel and supplant his identity such that, rather than a creative subject, we find an individual who lives in permanent melancholic revolt, *ressentiment,* and reaction against a perceived harm done.

§

To approach absurdity as a way of relating to objects in the inner world projected outward, rather than as an objective description of the world outside and its constituent parts reflected upon internally, is to imagine that absurdity describes a psychic posture involving certain dynamics operating within individuals or groups.

A careful look at this idea suggests that "absurdity" resembles "outrage," which derives from the Old French *outrage,* and the Latin *ultra* + *agium* (Campbell 1998, 116), meaning that which is *outré,* beyond or outside. Although, etymologically speaking, the term "outrage" has nothing to do with "rage," there is a kind of rage involved in designating something an "outrage."

When an offending person or thing is declared an "outrage," it is designated outside of the bounds of reason or acceptability, as if by means of an intellectual exile we defended ourselves from, and perhaps avenged, its affront. When something has scandalized our "sensibilities," we find it outrageous (*outré*-geous) and, in doing so, we relegate it to a separate, exogenous category. We make it foreign, alien, incomprehensible.

We cast objects outside of the realm of meaning, recognition, comprehension, and communication when we say, "This loss is not understandable but absurd." At the same time, we find a means to connect with our own overwhelming rage and grief. We sacrifice our ability to mourn the loss of these objects, to make meaning from their absence or silence or badness, in order to take up a position of psychological revolt and melancholic communion with our own anger at having been rejected, hurt, or deprived. As I have sought to demonstrate elsewhere (e.g., Bowker 2011; 2013; 2014; 2019), the absurd posture readily becomes one of permanent rage and perpetual grieving that may even insist upon the imposition of rage, loss, and grief upon others in the name of solidarity.

It can be fairly said of Camus that the thrust of his *oeuvre* is a multi-faceted attack on an abandoning or depriving agent. Camus rails against "the world," at powers that be, and even, at times, at God, for not being present, for not responding to our cries for help, for not bestowing on us what we need to make our lives worth living (1991b, 2–15). In this sense, Camus's work is about the unattained privilege of feeling "at home" in the world and, therefore, of being capable of living with the "ontological security" needed to make life meaningful (Laing 1969, 33).

Those who believe they are "at home" have chiefly lied to themselves, according to Camus, have taken an unjustifiable "leap of faith," or have otherwise betrayed a truth they know or ought to know about life and about themselves: that human beings can never be "at home" in the world, barring some kind of help that is lacking. Thus, those who claim to be at home provoke rage and envy for enjoying or pretending to enjoy a comfort we lack. With only a few exceptions (see, e.g., Camus 1995), Camus wrote of this privilege of being "at home" not in a literal sense, but in a broader, philosophical one.

§

Over the past several years (see, e.g., Bowker 2014; 2016; 2019b), I have argued that Camus's absurd posture and ambivalent attachment to the idea of "home" lay at the root of his most scandalous political stance, his rejection of complete Algerian independence from France. Camus's reasoning boiled down to the fact that the descendants of European colonists in Algeria (such as himself) were not guilty for having been born there. Since Algerian independence and self-determination would likely have required the displacement of these immigrants and their families, robbing them of their connection to their home, Camus held that absolute autonomy for Algeria was untenable. While

Camus was right that the ancestors of colonial occupants need not bear guilt for the actions of those who preceded them, it did not obviously follow that the pursuit of a reasonable and just solution to a complex political dilemma may not require them to suffer, just as autochthonous Algerians suffered mightily under French occupation.

Camus, a highly influential public figure on this subject, could well have advocated for measures that would have mitigated the negative impacts of Algerian independence on the descendants and families of European colonists. Instead, it seemed as if his ambivalent attraction to and rejection of the idea of finding a "home" in the world led him to support a continued but mitigated French colonial presence, effectively denying the native Algerian people the opportunity for full political self-determination.

If absurd protest refuses separateness, communication, and help in favor of melancholic revolt and rage, then its moral and political platforms will distract us from the most urgent necessities, such as recognizing and confronting obvious injustices, making reasonable and meaningful assessments of present-day dilemmas, and offering political and moral judgments while accepting necessary consequences of those judgments.

Instead, the vision of political community and identity advanced by Camus with respect to Algeria bore an uncanny resemblance to those totalizing ideologies Camus rejected throughout his life. That is, Camus demurred on the most difficult political realities while holding up a rather bizarre ideal of a shared, Mediterranean, "ur-cultural" identity (see, e.g., Carroll 1997, 529; Apter 1997, 508) to deny the need for Algerian independence.

Indeed, for Camus, it seemed, at least in his more abstract writings on the subject, that any community could be formed so long as it *shared* an experience of suffering (1991b, 14–22). Communities, then, need not be founded upon the codification of relationships based upon identities, attachments, or shared purposes, but, simply, "upon rebellion" (21), which generates an "awareness [...] no matter how confused it may be" of our basic connectedness (14).

It is this "metaphysical" solidarity that Camus defends quite often, in which "a man identifies himself with other men and so surpasses himself" in order to establish "the kind of solidarity that is born in chains" (17). For Camus, "the first progressive step for a mind overwhelmed by the strangeness of things is to realize that this feeling of strangeness is shared with all men and that human reality, in its entirety, suffers from the distance which separates it from the rest of the universe. *The malady experienced by a single man becomes a mass plague*" (22, emphasis added).

Community and solidarity seem to be found primarily or exclusively in *identification* — which Freud understood as the most primitive and "earliest emotional tie with another person" (1959, 37). Unfortunately, rather than emphasizing the (re-) cognition, communication, and relatedness of the separate and often incommensurable needs of distinct persons and parties, Camus's political theory seems an attempt to found a community on the grounds of shared meaninglessness.

This ideal of communion through suffering and strangeness, as I have tried to demonstrate elsewhere (Bowker 2014; 2016), is echoed throughout postmodern and contemporary ethics, in which subjectivity and recognition are rejected in favor of group membership founded upon a "*point of identification with suffering itself*" (Butler 2004, 30, emphasis added). Both the absurd and the postmodern vision of community, then, present real obstacles to the contemporary imagination of meaningful (re-) cognition, inter-subjectivity, and communication as moral and political values.

For those who are missing the capacities to find or create homes for themselves, efforts to establish a home in world outside take the shape of an ambivalently driven search for the lost home and for the lost objects that would have secured that home. The search for a new home in a new world is ambivalently driven because the goal is both to recover the home and to destroy the home. It may even take the shape of destroying the homes of others, so as to return to an internal state of being that is not safe but is, at least, familiarly dangerous.

These complex quests for a home, rather than engendering nurturing attitudes toward the self and others and a shared recognition of their need to create places where children can safely develop into autonomous persons, all too readily impels those engaged with it to adopt destructive, paranoid orientations and "mental constellation[s] of revolt" toward external representatives of internal objects that make life in the home absurd, if not dangerous. In "revolting" against the unjust distribution of privilege, one may even end by unconsciously taking up (re-enacting) the role of the depriving and oppressing agent one consciously rejects.

§

If Camus's "absurd man is the contrary of the reconciled man" (1991b, 59n), and if his aim, in a world perceived to be pervaded by victimization, violence, and loss, is not to recover meaning and wholeness but merely "to live with [his] ailments" (38), then only by perpetuating a condition of disrupted being can the absurd rebel find his innocence. Only in a survival scenario where all are constantly under threat of extinction is the absurd rebel able to suppress the temptation to assert subjectivity, announce values, make history, and live creatively, not in the sense of a creative artist, but in the sense elucidated by the psychoanalyst D.W. Winnicott (1986), where mature creativity requires a more or less integrated self, not one preoccupied with rage or revolt.

The absurd stance, while seeming to rebel against a bad object, actually replicates key components of the bad object's violence, particularly its extremity. The absurd actor must destroy the enemy and then destroy himself, so that *all* guilt and badness are erased from memory. One way to understand this unfortunate repetition is to recall that a substantial part of what makes a "bad" object "bad," in formative experience, is that the bad object represents a lie. The lie of the bad object is that it promises care and gratification but delivers pain and deprivation. For Camus and others, conforming to reality by understanding it, by "living with it" in a figurative sense, or by justifying it and making it appear to be "good," means lying about the realities of pain and deprivation, consenting to them as if they were help and gratification.

However, for Camus, it would seem that this lie has come to represent *all* that is bad about the bad object. That is, the badness of bad objects and bad acts are found not in their violence but in our comprehension of their violence. Real violence and destructiveness are attended to less than the self's symbolic, psychological, and internal negotiations with the ideas of violence and destructiveness. Badness is thereby displaced from the violent act and actor onto the self that might justify the act, rationalize violence, or otherwise partake in what absurd and postmodern rebels consider to be cruel illusions of care, justice, or progress.

§

Perhaps there is no more appropriate term than "absurd" to describe our horror and outrage at Auschwitz, or at the Nazi guard who famously told Primo Levi that "here there is no why [*hier gibt es kein warum*]" (Levi 1996, 29). Because shock, confusion, and senselessness already pervade such horrors, we may be reluctant to give them up. Declaring such events to be absurd both contains and distances us from their injustice, inhumanity, and terror.

What Camus seems to say of such events is that they force us to contend with losses so great we have no recourse but to find them absurd, lest we lose some important part of what makes us human. To mourn, to heal, and to move on from these tragedies, Camus and others seem to say, would be to accept them, which, in turn, would normalize them, integrate them into the fabric of everyday life. Camus seemed to recognize that the fight against absurdity is itself absurd, because we declare Auschwitz absurd today to protest Auschwitz's occurrence yesterday, which is quixotic but understandable as a psychological stance that will not tolerate the acceptance or assimilation of the losses of life, humanity, and moral limits that Auschwitz implies.

We may be terrified of assimilating such losses because we are terrified of getting used to them, of being connected to them, in no small part because we fear that to do so would invite their repetition. If the posture of absurdity permits such losses never to be fully understood, and therefore never to be fully mourned, it also permits us to experience ourselves as largely innocent combatants against those who instigated them.

Nevertheless, read in this light, absurdity becomes a protest not against violence but against *comprehending* violence, the comprehension of loss and violence associated with rationalization or habituation that covers them up, often by declaring loss and violence necessary or understandable in the context of its causes or intentions. In rebelling against the comprehension of loss and violence, the absurd rebel ends up rebelling against the ability to make them meaningful and the ability to live through them, and even live beyond them, as subjects.

By equating meaning, understanding, mourning, and thinking with collaboration, conformity, and complicity in violence, such perspectives terrorize understanding and being by forcing the self into an absurd dilemma whereby its abilities

to comprehend, contend with, and "live with" badness and violence become affronts to its innocence. Perhaps, like Camus's relative utopianism, such perspectives are not so bold as to seek "a world in which murder no longer exists" (1991a, 120–21).[4] What is troubling is that, in the place of a world without violence, we should seek a world in which a form of psychological

4   In the short essay, "To Save Lives," Camus offered a theoretical frame for his 'relative utopianism': "People like myself want not a world where murder no longer exists (we are not so crazy as that!), but one where murder is no longer legitimized. Here we are indeed utopian — and contradictorily so. For we live in a world where murder is legitimized, and if we do not like that, we must change it… In a more relative utopia, we could demand that murder be no longer legitimized" (1991a, 120–21).

violence and self-violence is used as a tool to destroy meaningful doing and being.

Most who write of the Holocaust qualify their work by asserting that the experience can never be completely understood. Some even argue that what makes the Holocaust unique is that "what occurred in Nazi death camps was so absolutely evil that, like no other event in human history, *it defies human capacities for understanding*" (Neiman 2002, 2, emphasis added). Such claims arise from an absurd protest against the Holocaust's horrors. We are mystified not only out of respect for all those who suffered so immensely, but because our mystification is an integral part of our protest.

But does calling Auschwitz "absurd" make the suffering of the victims of the Holocaust more meaningful? Does it prepare us to live and struggle against future atrocities or does it only offer shallow reassurance that, as long as one remains mystified by loss, all is not lost? Perhaps there are sufferings so great, so threatening even to witness or contemplate, that our ability to make them meaningful should be revoked in protest. In this spirit we may understand Claude Lanzmann's declaration that "there is an absolute obscenity in the very project of understanding" the Holocaust (1995, 204). Theodor Adorno's famous statement that poetry after Auschwitz would be barbaric and Primo Levi's claim that, "if for no other reason than that an Auschwitz existed, no one in our age should speak of Providence" (1996, 157–58), express a sentiment that is not entirely dissimilar.

The real question of absurdity is the question of whether people like Lanzmann, Adorno, and Levi are right. Taken together, our projects of understanding, poetry, and Providence compose much of our ability to accept loss, to assimilate loss, to make loss meaningful. Refusing understanding, therefore, protects our outrage as one small thing that can never be lost, but it also requires that our outrage can never be resolved, that reality can never be comprehensible or meaningful, and that while we may revolt in order to be a part of a collectivity, we must sacrifice our ability to be mature adults.

Courage Doesn't Help

Helping every feeble neighbor,
Seeking help from none...
Kindness in another's trouble,
Courage in your own.

— Adam Lindsay Gordon, 1893

The concepts of courage and bravery have become so much a part of common language that they are often applied to situations in which they stand out as wildly inappropriate, especially when given a closer look. For instance, the headline, "Brave one-year-old undergoes successful heart transplant operation" (Scarre 2010, 30), would be difficult to defend if its attribution of bravery were examined thoughtfully.

While there are important distinctions between bravery and, say, heroism, differences between bravery and courage tend to be semantic or arbitrary. One might take as an example Warshaw's brief (2019) article on the difference between bravery and courage, where bravery is defined as "the ability to confront something painful or difficult or dangerous without any fear," while courage is understood as "the ability to confront something painful or difficult or dangerous *despite* any fear" (emphasis in original).

Much of what has been written about the relationship between anxiety and courage should disturb those with psychoanalytic sympathies, mainly because these literatures often
endorse a defensive externalization of anxiety and a form of
magical thinking. Often praised for its ability to afford human
beings the "opportunity" to act courageously, for Paul Tillich,
anxiety is precisely the opportunity to enact "the courage to
be," which entails "resist[ing] the radical threat of nonbeing," by
rejecting the "courage of despair" and attending to the "meaningful attempt to reveal the meaninglessness of our situation"
(1952, 140). For Rollo May, anxiety is a boon because it gives
us a chance to act courageously and in freedom, by which May
means — surprisingly — to transform our amorphous anxieties
into manageable fears of identifiable objects, and then to avoid
them or to stand against them in such a way as to reduce fearful
experiences (1950).

More recently, Coline Covington has argued that "being true
to oneself is at the core of bravery [for Covington, bravery and
courage are identical] and is the common factor in each act of
bravery" (2021, xvii). Standing against "prevailing political forces," bravery is, then, "the opposite of evil" because it requires
only being "true to oneself" (xvi). Here, too, we see an externalizing of the feared (evil) objects and a questionable connection
between being one's true self and an external combat against
external ills.

A related understanding of anxiety and courage is cham-
pioned by advocates of exposure therapy and others, such as
Sherry Armatinstein (2021), who, in offering "tips to overcoming anxiety and phobias," argues that

> it is human nature to avoid emotions that scare us… Except
> that by continually avoiding looking at the 'boogeyman'
> within, you become hostage to the monster. Typically, this
> involves hiding from any potential stressor that might cause
> upset and engaging in endless distractions… The good news
> is that once you face your fear [*note that it is not one's anxiety*

that is faced] — and give the boogeyman air — rather than shove it into a distant compartment of your brain, it begins losing the ability to rule you and dictate your decisions.

We commonly think of courage as overcoming fear to accomplish something meaningful in the world. The literatures and discourses cited above suggest that courage may be, instead, an externalizing defense against internal anxiety. In other words, "[t]o rid oneself of anxiety, find a suitable external fear that can be face and make it manifest in the world," as Armatinstein recommends. Once the experience of anxiety is made external and bounded, then it can be faced according to the dictates of external reality. But of course what is avoided is precisely the internal reality of a crisis.

To be sure, there are several discourses about courage (e.g., historical, political, feminist) aside from those which I have cited. Sadly, it is beyond the scope of this essay to review the extensive literatures on the subject, from Plato's day to the present (for excellent beginnings, see Mackenzie 1962; Scarre 2010; Walton 1986). It suffices to say that, in most cases, courage and bravery are valorized as a means by which experiences of anxiety may be transformed into something positive in the world, primarily because we wish them to be.

Involved in this assertion, then, is a kind of magical thinking: for instance, the belief that "being oneself" combats "evil" in the world. But, of course, this magical power is, in actuality, little more than a projection of inner angst onto external objects or others. Indeed, like Covington's "prevailing political forces," Tillich externalizes his fear and hatred upon what he describes as an uncourageous (existentialist) lot who "are unable to understand what is happening in our period" (1952, 140).

Such considerations leave us with a vision of courage that seems, frankly, quite *uncourageous* in its refusal to contend seriously with the experience of anxiety itself. Instead, in what would seem to be a well-organized defense against anxiety, these approaches are attempts to dislodge anxiety from the anxious self, either by making that self a part of our anxious species-being (see, e.g., Heidegger 1962), or by contending that anxiety may be magically transposed into fears of palpable objects which may be confronted or "faced."

An interesting example of courage in this respect is the oft-cited 1943 defacing of the Feldherrnhalle, bastion of Nazi power and authority, by the White Rose student opposition group. This act has been described as one of "outstanding courage" as well as one "plainly [...] calling for the most exceptional bravery" (Scarre 2010, 1–2). This defiant vandalism of one of Hitler's most sacred shrines (while perhaps doing little to halt Nazi aggression throughout Europe) may be understood as a metaphorical expression of externalized anxiety.

The helplessness of students, like that of many citizens and groups in Germany, before the Nazi rise to power, generated profound anxiety and even shame, rooted in the perceived inability to defend oneself and others. It is a point of interest that the action was not precisely one of destruction but rather of "de-face-ing." Here, we see an effort to strip some of the veneer of power and authority from the Nazi party by causing it to "lose face," as it were. Even members of the White Rose group, such as Christoph Probst, criticized the students' vandalism as a "pointless escapade" (see Dumbach and Newborn 2006, 140–41), whereas, from the psychological standpoint I have briefly constructed above, the act fulfills its (internal) mission, which is to externalize the shame and ugliness of helplessness into an outcry (a crying out) that receives attention, even if the attention is ultimately negative.

§

Many courage discourses ask us to do the needful, to "be afraid [of something] and do it anyway" and "to do what needs to be done in spite of fear" (Peterson and Seligman, 2004, 199), particularly when that action is required or desired by others. In this case, individuals are asked to set aside their fears — including their fear of being harmed or killed — for the sake of an object with which they identify and upon identification with which they depend. The paradigmatic example of this type of courage is the soldier who throws himself on a grenade, killing himself but absorbing the impact of the explosion to preventing his comrades from harm.

Curious is that many persons describe such putatively courageous acts as deriving from an alignment with social norms and values, primarily with "adherence to values, beliefs, and norms that were internalized, adopted as one's own, and/or developed in the course of experience" (Staub 1979, 11). The Oliners, in their famous study of those who helped Jews during the Nazi occupation of Europe, found no subjects who cited courage as a motivating factor in their actions. Instead, respondents recalled parents who had "emphasized moral values as guidelines for future behavior and as being emotionally warm and caring individuals" (Nadler 2020, 58), what they call a "normocentric" motivation "rooted [...] in a feeling of obligation to a social reference group with whom the actor identifies and whose explicit and implicit rules he feels obliged to obey" (Oliner and Oliner 1988, 188–89). Others understand their own brave acts as acts of madness (Scarre 2010, 159–60n).

Here, it would seem to be anxiety, not fear, that arises internally when faced with danger. The danger most pressing seems to be the prospect of violating core, internalized values. And here, too, courage discourses would utterly miss the point that courage, in such cases, involves the dread of the loss of identification with the good object rather than an overcoming of fear. In Winnicottian language, we might even say that courage appears as a giving way to the false self, to the self that adapts and conforms to the demands and desires of other persons and groups.

In general, theoretical discourses of courage and anxiety do not match up with lived experience. Philip Larkin's poem, *"Aubade"* (2011), captures the situation well. Against that anxiety which "stays just on the edge of vision [...] a standing chill [...]

Courage is no good:
It means not scaring others. Being brave
Lets no one off the grave.

In living with our anxieties,

[…] telephones crouch, getting ready to ring
In locked-up offices, and all the uncaring
Intricate rented world begins to rouse.
The sky is white as clay, with no sun.
Work has to be done.
Postmen like doctors go from house to house.

Our anxiety remains, yet there is nothing (*no thing*) to fear. Life goes on and the "world begins to rouse," our daily work resumes and "postmen […] go from house to house."

§

As we have discussed, most courage discourses suggest a fixation on external objects of fear and external crisis. But the crises on which we fixate are rarely the real crises that have motivated our fixation. Of course, they may be "real" enough, in the sense that real others (or we, ourselves) may be harmed or even killed, but these external crises very often refer us back to an experience of internal crisis that occurred much earlier (see also "Trauma and the Self," this volume), when we were confronted with the possibility of psychic death or damage, an experience to which we had no adequate response but anxiety because we had no means of struggle, "nothing (*no thing*) to do."

Crisis may be understood as a state in which the individual can find no possible response. Crisis implies *stasis* in both the original and the casual uses of the term. It implies an extreme helplessness, at least inwardly. But it can also describe a state of frenetic activity, even though this activity is not likely to — and is frequently not even intended to — resolve the underlying predicament. For instance, when Kagan and Schlosberg describe families who are "addicted" to a state of perpetual crisis (1989), they mean both that there is a real, fundamental intra-psychic problem to be overcome (a real crisis, such as the past or present psychic death of one or both of the parents) and a false problem that is always being called forth, one that may symbolize the real crisis, but that is never linked up with the deeper problem.

In states of crisis, actions and speech are often placed on a combative moral plane. Another important reason why theoretical discourses of courage do not match up with lived experience is that most discourses of courage (see also Shklar 1989; Scorza 2001) do the same. In the (moral) combat against crisis, the reality of the self is obscured and an exaggerated solidity and integration are accounted to the self, one that selves rarely possess. Put another way, discourses of courage presume a non-problematic subject that is exactly what is missing if one must resort to the kind of defensive externalization and magical thinking cited above. Courage is, in this way, a defense and a retreat from unresolved anxiety, from an inner reality that is more disintegrated than the courageous stance implies. The "good and evil" political forces implicated in most courage discourses locate persons in a moral drama that shares many similarities with the dilemma of perpetual crisis and of the absurd. It simplifies the characters and their problems, necessitating an endless struggle in which one is destined to fail.

I would argue that anxiety, as opposed to fear, cannot be fought with courage. Indeed, these reflections help us understand why, while courage seems to have some important role in the discussion of fear, it has little place in serious discussions of anxiety. Since anxiety reflects a state of crisis in the inner world, there is no external object to fight and to serve as a vehicle for courage. Indeed, the best we can say is that not courage but mourning and integration are the work of the anxious self: that *integration is to anxiety what courage is to fear.*

§

Having argued that courage discourses draw attention away from the problem of anxiety, rather than addressing it, and that anxiety is internalized shame rooted in helplessness, a brief, concluding excursus on true helplessness and psychic death is needed. True helplessness would mean not only the impossibility of acting in the world but the impossibility of surviving psychically, for we begin with and remain dependent on others' help to support our identities, meanings, and attachments. Indeed, we may say that we need help to keep ourselves alive because aliveness means involving the self in projects in which the self's possibility is made real or actual.

Encounters with psychic death, then, are traumatic because they mean the end of possibility. To say as much is to say that in the state of psychic aliveness, one encounters possibility in a Kierkegaardian sense (1980). Psychic death is the threat of not being, not merely of dying and not only of being nothing, but rather of being *nothing but what one is,* of being a creature without possibility, and so of being lifeless and inert. The threat of psychic death is piqued when we are confronted with situations where nothing is possible for us, when there is nothing to do, when we are unable to act, as in anxiety as well as crisis.

The capacity to imagine and create possibility, and then to make the possible actual, contains within it, on one hand, overwhelming potential and existential freedom. On the other hand, we face the prospect of *not* coming into being, of *not* making the possible actual, or of succumbing to a world in which nothing is possible for us.

To begin to resolve this dilemma ultimately requires an acknowledgment of one's incompleteness and vulnerability within certain limits. These limits are defined by the self's ability to rely on internalized helpers (internalized good objects) to "help itself" in times of need. That is, it takes the integration and acceptance of both contingencies, possibility and impossibility, rather than courage, to begin to face our anxiety at a fundamental level.

Anxiety

The only sure way to address anxiety is to write about it during a period of extreme anxiety. This is what I am doing, although I find immediately that it is difficult to write about the experience, even or especially when one is going through it. This difficulty has something important to do with the nature of anxiety.

Anxiety lives outside of any system of meaning because anxiety is related to the helplessness we feel when our systems of meaning break down. Thus, anxiety may not be beyond language altogether, but it may be beyond the language of the one experiencing anxiety, since it is his conceptual world that is falling apart.

From my hospital journal:

I am so sad and so frightened, like a child. What is at the bottom of this? A lack of trust? A belief that I will break down and fail and bring pain and shame to myself and my family? Why do I have that belief? Because it is not a belief but a feeling. This is why CBT won't help me.

I am struggling to find myself, and amidst all of this change, I feel lost… What is the fear? When I wake up, what is it I am afraid of? Nothing? Uncertainty? I am afraid of breaking my life and those around me, of breaking into catastrophe. Why am I afraid of catastrophe? It is beyond my ability to express. Can anything help me if I can't even describe the problem?

It is a kind of trauma to receive something other than help when help is needed.

It is interesting how people respond to cries for help. Often with defensiveness, as if the helplessness of the sufferer needed to be warded off.

A helper self and a helped self map on pretty well to Winnicott's true and false selves, which, we have to remember, are part of a defensive organization:

> *in which there is a premature taking over of the nursing functions of the mother, so that the infant or child adapts to the environment while at the same time protecting and hiding the true self, or the source of personal impulses (1989, 43).[1]*

The helper self, in cases of psychic disturbance, has had to decipher or discover means of helping himself as replacements for the help of the parent.

But this means the helper self can be a part of the false-self system. Can it not also be part of a healthy maturation process that leads to autonomy? Yes, but for this to happen, it must not be called on too early after a disruption, as it does not yet have its bearings.

Maybe anxiety is the failure of this helper self even to make articulate what is happening to the self, its own helplessness amidst its idiosyncratic chaos. That would be Ramon Guthrie's argument (1968, 31), I think:

---

1   For my second trip to the hospital, I had the presence of mind to bring a copy of Winnicott's *Psychoanalytic Explorations* (1989).

No, lady, the foregoing poem is neither
a riddle nor a rebus. Nothing to be guessed.
When it says, "It has no name," it means just that.
No, not "grace," "vision," "caritas,"
or some exuberant, all-embracing, new,
exhilarating virtue that God and I
have just concocted. [...]

                                        Listen ...
No, that is asking too much. Even as I set to speak,
you gasp, "How fascinating it must be to live
in that mind of yours where everything
is glistening new and subtle and alive!
I often wonder what it must be like."

Hold tight! I am about to tell you. Mostly,
it is like being a nightwatchman in a morgue
where it is always night and all of the cadavers
suffer from perpetual insomnia
even in their most excruciating nightmares,
while he himself lives in continual sick dread
of being fired.

§

Sometimes I feel that I have it good, that my loved ones are
wonderful, that I am terribly lucky, but this does nothing, surprisingly, to alleviate panic or anxiety. If anything, the contrast
between how I think I should feel and how I do feel only creates
guilt and makes things more painful.

*I already have God's love or I don't. What I want now is God's
help.*

Anxiety expresses a lack of faith in help: that neither any other nor the world itself can be counted on to help us feel safe. Thus, while we do not encounter all dangers alone, if we are anxious, we encounter all dangers helplessly.

§

Anxiety is an experience of helplessness. Anxiety is about fear of loss of control (past, present, or future).

A world without control is an anxious world in which danger is ever-present and no one is capable of helping. The only reasonable orientation to such a world is paranoia and, to some degree, splitting, to protect the precious few good things in the dangerous world from the immensity of the intractable bad. The loss of any interpretive context or system of meaning in which one can be oneself returns one to a primitive system of meaning, perhaps even more primitive than the Kleinian paranoid-schizoid position.

Anxiety is about having done or been something, or becoming something in the future, and being helpless to alter its course. This is more than just the psychoanalytic truism that what is feared has *already* occurred. What truly makes a person anxious is the belief that the anxiety, itself, is but an expression of the badness that already lies within.

If a person is inclined to moral or religious thinking — and aren't we all to some extent or other, especially when pressed — then anxiety may take the form of "punishment" for "offense" or "sin" even if the individual is not quite certain what offense or sin has been committed.

Perhaps that is the key about anxiety. It seems to draw one to the conclusion that one has done something wrong and unforgiveable. Why else would one feel this way?

The persistence of anxiety suggests that it is not merely a fleeting worry about an acute, discrete, or concrete event or situation but rather a kind of communication between the self and itself that holds moral judgment. Judgment because anxiety is among the purest forms of psychological pain.

Why is pain needed? What exactly makes one deserving of such pain? It is the self who delivers the pain, and surely the self is not a capricious judge and jury, i.e., there must be some *reason* for all the agony, we think. Having lost the reasons means having lost control (again and again) over one's universe and over one's experience of meaningful things, things that make sense.

Anxiety is also the part of us that hopes for help, a hope that threatens to destroy the world. It emerges, as in attachment theory, alongside ambivalence and so a Kleinian way of understanding development lends itself nicely to this way of thinking. The anxious part of the self is pulled toward a paranoid-schizoid orientation and cannot find a way to reach the depressive position, as integrated love for the attachment figure is made impossible because of the conflict between the part of the self that both hopes for reparation and the part of the self that refuses to make reparations or to permit reparations to occur. In the paranoid-schizoid position, anxiety anticipates abandonment, the loss of all good, and helplessness in the face of threats.

One way of saying this would be: Anxiety expresses the helplessness of the self, combined with the refusal to give up hope for help. Of course, whether or not one should give up hope for help depends entirely on whether one is speaking about external figures who may or may not change their behavior or about what ultimately facilitates or obstructs help: the internal forces and objects and their (unreliable, neglectful, hurtful) character.

Hikikomori, Amae, and Help

Hikikomori (ひきこもり) derives from the Japanese words *hiku* (引く, "pulling in") and *komoru* (こもる, "retiring"). It means, literally, "pulling away and being confined" (Hairston 2010, 311; Lee 2009, 128), or "to be confined to the inside" (Ohashi 2008, iii), and is used to refer to the state of isolation ("to be in *hikikomori*") as well as the affected individual ("a *hikikomori*"). The construct, which describes a period of social isolation often lasting for several years, has gained widespread notoriety in Japan and worldwide since the year 2000. It was first introduced to the Japanese lexicon in 1998 with the publication of Tamaki Saitō's book, *Social Withdrawal* [社会的ひきこもり, *Shakaiteki Hikikomori*]. New estimates suggest that millions of individuals, in Japan and beyond (Bowker et al. 2019), will suffer from *hikikomori* in their lifetimes.

In spite of numerous attempts to define and classify the phenomenon, there remains an astounding degree of confusion regarding *hikikomori*. One finds at every turn "conflicting results and lack of empirical findings on risk factors" (Umeda and Kawakami 2012, 121), such that even the most fundamental elements of the condition remain in question. Some of the difficulty in defining *hikikomori* surely results from challenges associated with studying a population that is, by definition, *highly averse to seeking help*. Individuals in *hikikomori* present themselves for help rarely and with seemingly little insight into their own experience. A common response when asked what caused an individual's period of *hikikomori,* or what the experience was like, is: "I don't know" (Kato et al. 2012, 1063; Jones 2006).

Japanese individuals in *hikikomori,* upon whom more has been written in recent years than upon agoraphobics or socially isolated individuals in any other country, have received a predominantly negative treatment in the Japanese media and public (Hattori 2005; Kitayama et al. 2001). The broader Japanese public, writes Yuichi Hattori, remains "hostile to *Hikikomori* and assumes that it is a moral weakness, rather than a legitimate psychological disorder […]. The man or woman on the street regards people with *Hikikomori* as spoiled, lazy young people who willfully disregard their parents' wishes and arbitrarily avoid social obligations" (2005, 198).

Although depictions of *hikikomori* in youth-directed media may be sympathetic, films such as *Hikikomori: Tokyo Plastic* (2004), which depicts a cruel *hikikomori* operating from his solitary lair who corrupts and endangers two young women, are not uncommon. *Hikikomori*'s pejorative connotations are also inseparable from its introduction to the Japanese public via two widely publicized crimes committed by men in *hikikomori,* one involving the hijacking of a bus and the killing of a passenger, the other involving the kidnapping and extended captivity of a child (Rees 2002).

While attempts have been made to change the perception of *hikikomori,* and while more treatment centers have become available, some radical responses suggest the presence of widespread fear and hatred of *hikikomori* and what it represents. One "recovery" organization was recently sued for having run "an 'abduction and confinement' regime" in which a detainee died after being "chained to a pillar for four days" (Furlong 2008, 317). Similarly, in the early days of moral panic regarding the condition, unofficial "boot-camp facilities" were established in which "parents coerce[d] youth with *Hikikomori* into military-like training programs," where they were "forced to perform manual labor for disciplinary purposes" (Hattori 2005, 198). Although condemned for their actions, such organizations apparently "received an enormous amount of sympathy from a public who regard *hikikomori* as free-riding parasites and feel that parents are not providing the discipline necessary to reform this anti-social behaviour" (Furlong 2008, 317).

Today, efforts to soften the perception of *hikikomori* coincide with scholarly attempts to relate *hikikomori* to mood, personality, or anxiety disorders (see, e.g., Kondo et al. 2011; Nagata et al. 2011), and to examine "instances" of *hikikomori* in other countries (see, e.g., Teo 2012; Sakamoto et al. 2005). Such attempts have met with mixed results and even with resistance from the researchers themselves, who almost universally maintain that *hikikomori* is a "culture-bound syndrome," unique to Japan. Indeed, a review of literature on the subject makes it impossible to avoid the conclusion that, in spite of the proliferation of empirical articles and reports, progress in understanding *hikikomori* is at a standstill. This standstill is not for a lack of data, lack of attention, or lack of effort. Rather, I believe that the lack of progress in interpreting *hikikomori* reflects a multi-faceted resistance in which both individuals in *hikikomori* and those who study and treat them participate.

§

Mystification, a Marxist term popularized in psychoanalytic theory by R.D. Laing (1964; 1985), means to confuse and disorient, to prevent understanding, or to impose a false reality upon others in order to prevent their recognition of some aspect of experience relevant to the self. Mystification may involve the use of both subtle and overt forms of aggression to protect a cherished belief or fantasy that would be lost if subjected to conscious scrutiny. Laing notes that mystification primarily involves the abuse of others to shore up the self's repressive efforts, since "if the one person does not want to know something or to remember something, it is not enough to repress it (or otherwise 'successfully' defend himself against it 'in' himself); he must not be reminded of it by the other" (1985, 348).

A host of fearsome consequences await the one who attempts to break through the veil of mystification. The skeptic, the whistle-blower, the dissident, or the analyst who questions the false reality protected by mystification may be cast as irresponsible, cruel, heretical, aggressive, insane, and the like. In most cases, the resistance to penetrating what has been mystified is grounded not primarily in reasonable fears about likely negative consequences, but in unconscious associations and ancient terrors of bad objects that mis-represented and mis-figured themselves (i.e., mystified themselves) as good.

Interpreting the scholarly and clinical literatures on *hikikomori* with an eye to defensive resistance proves to be a helpful method of approaching the phenomenon of *hikikomori* itself. Of course, understanding psychosocial phenomena like *hikikomori* in their proper context is often valuable, but in this case, a sort of intellectual protectionism of *hikikomori* has mystified rather than illuminated the condition. At the same time, in spite of insistences that researchers focus on culturally unique interpretive keys, the most relevant of Japanese socio-cultural norms, *amae* (甘え) (maternal help and indulgence), has been consistently mistaken and misapplied.

After examining the mystifying effects on the literatures on *hikikomori,* I suggest an interpretation of *hikikomori,* itself, as a conflict between hope and shame concerning the desire to be helped. To do so, I rely on Franz Kafka's famous short story, *Die Verwandlung* (*The Metamorphosis*)*,* as well as D.W. Winnicott's conception of the relationship between deprivation and delinquency to show that the attempt to recover *amae,* while holding the belief that such desire is shameful or even "monstrous," explains the complex combination of hope, self-deprivation, and victimization at the root of the *hikikomori* phenomenon.

§

It is beyond the scope of this essay to review the extensive literature that contests the viability of the concept of "culture" (see, e.g., Finkielkraut 1987; Eagleton 2000). It is undeniable, however, that in the realm of the social and behavioral sciences "culture" has often served a less-than-noble function, tending to promote stereotyping, chauvinism, and orientalism (see Said 1979), as much or more than meaningful understandings. In the domain of psychology, Ethan Watters quips that the so-called "culture-bound syndromes" treated so delicately in the final pages of the *DSM* [*Diagnostic and Statistical Manual of Mental Disorders*], such as koro and amok, are for the reader little more than "carnival sideshows" that "might as well be labeled 'Psychiatric Exotica: Two Bits a Gander'" (2010, 5).

While it is not classified in the *DSM-V* or *ICD* [*International Classification of Diseases*], *hikikomori* is recognized by mental health organizations and research institutions around the world as a "culture-bound syndrome." While acknowledging the flaws of the term, and while recognizing the existence of similar if not identical phenomena in other countries, Teo, Stufflebaum, and Kato (2014) argue that *hikikomori* must be considered a "culture-bound syndrome" because "(i) it is a discrete, well-defined syndrome; (ii) it has been argued as a specific illness; (iii) it is expected, recognized and to some degree sanctioned as a response to certain cultural precipitants; and (iv) it has a higher incidence of prevalence [in Japan] compared to other cultures" (449).

Although there are competing theories concerning the nature and cause of *hikikomori,* Jonathan Watts remains correct that "there is broad agreement that this illness is a product of the affluence, technology, and convenience of modern Japanese life" (2002, 1131). That is, while not ignoring "wider sociological trends," such as "the breakdown of communication and collapse of the family and human relations" in Japan (Allison 2013, 74), scholars and pundits turn most often for explanation to "the phenomenal growth of the Japanese economy during the latter half of the 20th century and the tremendous technologi-cal progress the country made during that time" (Murakami 2000; Kato et al. 2011, 67). At a national or cultural level, then, *hikikomori* is thought to represent "a disease born of prosper-ity" (Zielenziger 2006), reflecting excess, privilege, permissive-ness, and the indulgence of youth. This claim corresponds well with those who believe that individuals in *hikikomori* have been spoiled by the Japanese parenting culture, which includes the tradition of *amae,* to be discussed in even more detail below.

For the moment, however, we must consider that, regard-less of the nature or cause of *hikikomori,* if *hikikomori* is to be defined as a Japanese phenomenon, then it is comprehensible only within the context of Japanese social, cultural, and famil-ial affairs. And while scholars continue to debate the details of the phenomenon, few have recognized the consequences of ap-proaching *hikikomori* as a "culture-bound syndrome" itself. To define *hikikomori* as a syndrome that "thrives in one particular country during a particular moment in its history" (Jones 2006) is to insist upon a very specific relationship between it and con-temporary Japanese culture. This means that *hikikomori,* and all it represents, is excluded from explanation via theories and constructs that are not specific to Japan (e.g., agoraphobia or social withdrawal) and that are not culturally oriented (e.g., ex-planations that focus on intrapsychic factors or early childhood experience).

Even among Japanese clinicians and researchers, there seems to be a resistance to theorizing the phenomenon and to hypoth-esizing its meaning. International studies have found that Japa-nese psychiatrists tend to attribute *hikikomori* to a wide array of (often vague) social and cultural factors much more often than psychiatrists from other countries. This tendency has led many Japanese care-providers "to be more passive in providing medical intervention in *hikikomori* cases," perhaps indicating a reluctance to act given the clinical and medical uncertainty sur-rounding the nature of *hikikomori* and perhaps evincing a belief in the inevitability of *hikikomori* in Japan given its putative cultural entrenchment (Tateno et al. 2012, 4).

What is more, defining *hikikomori* as a culture-bound syndrome permits *hikikomori* to stand for a blanket social critique of Japanese society. Michael Zielenziger, for instance, has argued that young people in Japan "want to be different than their parents and different from their peers, but Japan is so collectively engineered that it's very difficult, if not impossible, for them to really express themselves" (2006). Similarly, in her article *"Hikikomania,"* Kathleen Todd argues that Japanese society has created a situation in which a young person's "original personality" is excluded, "while the front [false] personality compulsively conforms to perceived expectations" (2011, 137–38). While such critiques could hardly be more vague, and while they might as well be applied to most youth populations on the planet, the high rates of *hikikomori* in Japan seem to serve as anecdotal evidence in support of such claims.

If, as Judith Herman has argued, "every instance of severe traumatic psychological injury is a standing challenge to the rightness of the social order" (Shay 1995, 3), it is this belief that has made the concept of trauma so fascinating to social theorists in Europe and North America for the past three and a half decades. This same link — the link between the victims of a psychological syndrome and their potential use as fuel for a social or political critique — is part of what has made *hikikomori* such an attractive concept for the clinical, academic, and popular imagination both within Japan and beyond. Many wish to use *hikikomori* as a sign that something is amiss in Japanese society, but, in order to serve this function, the experience of *hikikomori* must be discussed but never pinned down, must be transmitted but not communicated, experienced but not understood. These considerations shed light on one salient aspect of the literature on *hikikomori* taken up below, the relationship between the refusal of understanding and a form of victimization.

The literature on *hikikomori* uses the self-punishment and self-deprivation of those suffering from the syndrome to direct criticism at the relatively easy targets of "Japanese society" and

"Japanese culture" and, in this way, finds what Vamik Volkan calls "suitable targets of externalization" for anger (1985). While individuals recovering from *hikikomori* have been known to express "detailed critique[s] of Japanese society" (Zielenziger 2006), the behavior typical of individuals in *hikikomori* suggests that their anger is directed at the family members whom they shut out and passively victimize. Nor is it clear to what extent broader social critiques reflect the individuals' experience of *hikikomori,* as opposed to the individual's eventual accommodation to the commonly accepted way of understanding his experience. It may be, for instance, that blaming Japanese society for the psychic pain associated with *hikikomori* is necessary for the individual to "recover" in Youth Support Centers and, more generally, in a culture that comprehends *hikikomori* symptoms along such lines.

In a moment, I turn briefly to Franz Kafka's famous story, *The Metamorphosis,* as a helpful fictional narrative by which to frame the complex experience of *hikikomori.* To my knowledge, no one has yet explored the relationship between *hikikomori* and Kafka's work (nor that of any other relevant non-Japanese writer concerned with isolation and solitude), likely because of the pervasive belief that such texts and their meanings are not relevant to the uniquely Japanese phenomenon. Protecting and isolating the *hikikomori* phenomenon, as it were, within Japan's cultural confines, therefore, signifies a restriction of the possibility of understanding and communicating about *hikikomori,* both within and outside of Japan. I hope to show that it is more than a simple irony that restrictions upon understanding and communication are, in fact, central to the phenomenon of *hikikomori* itself.

§

A careful reading of the scholarly and popular literatures makes it difficult to avoid the conclusion that those who treat and study *hikikomori* have psychologically identified with their subjects, such that explaining their behavior to non-*hikikomori* individuals comes to represent a betrayal of individuals in *hikikomori* and their experience. Perhaps like those students of the Jewish holocaust who, with Claude Lanzmann, feel that there is an "absolute obscenity in the project of understanding the holocaust" (1995, 204), those who forge identifications with individuals in *hikikomori* see themselves as privileged witnesses to a type of suffering which it is their obligation to protect and defend. Without trivializing the horrors of the Nazi camps, it may be said that the self-incarceration of the individual in *hikikomori* is akin to a private concentration camp, one whose secret sufferings are carefully guarded against outsiders' understandings (see also Bowker 2013).

An excellent example of this protective dynamic may be found in the acclaimed (2008) Japanese film, *Tobira no mukō* (扉の向こう, *The Other Side of the Door*), which borders on documentary, and which stars Kenta Nigishi, himself a recovering *hikikomori*. The film depicts the struggle of the Okada family and their son Hiroshi, a teenaged boy who, one day, enters his room and is hardly seen or heard by the audience again. The film illustrates the effects of Hiroshi's *hikikomori* on his mother, father, and younger brother, while introducing audiences to Sadatsugo Kudo, who plays himself, as the director of a local Youth Support Center.

The film's depiction of all characters is sympathetic, and yet Hiroshi's *hikikomori* is inscrutable to audiences who must guess what has precipitated his isolation, his experience of it, and when or how he might emerge from it. In many ways, it is really the audience who is left on "the other side of the door," helpless to see or understand Hiroshi except in a way that suggests the film's real intent: to *transmit,* rather than communicate, the frustration, confusion, and helplessness experienced by those confronting *hikikomori*. To see the film is to wonder why it is necessary that nothing about Hiroshi, and *hikikomori,* be understood. Indeed, one is left with the impression that *the denial of help in communication and understanding is Hiroshi's goal,* the goal of the film, the goal of many individuals in *hikikomori,* and, perhaps, the goal of scholarly and popular treatments of *hikikomori* as well.

If the individual in *hikikomori* mystifies himself, refuses to communicate, to be understood, and to give or receive help, and so do the researchers working in the cottage industry of *hikikomori* scholarship, then what exactly must be mystified in *hikikomori* and what is the psychic meaning of this mystification? An answer to these questions lies in a closer examination of the concept of *amae* and, strangely enough, in its consistent misapplication by researchers on *hikikomori.*

§

The Japanese term, *amae,* and the verb *amaeru* (甘える), are quite close to the English nouns "indulgence" and "help" and the verb forms "to indulge oneself"/"help oneself." In English, "indulgence" actually has a rather complex range of meanings that are largely pejorative, since, for instance, one may indulge oneself, one may indulge one's baser instincts, one may indulge another person against one's better judgment, and so on. In all cases, *amae* involves yielding or acceding to the desires or demands for help or accommodation of another. In Japan, and one might argue in many cultures, it is expected that an infant or child will *amaeru* to his parents: that he will indulge in their help. That is, the child is expected to permit himself to become dependent upon his parents, to expect (as a *given*) his parents' adaptation to his needs and desires, and to enjoy this experience of help — at first unknowingly, but in time with some recognition of his state. It is also expected that the child's parents will not refuse or reject his dependence, and that a good many indulgences will be offered to the child. And the parent, of course, comes to depend upon the child's dependence, and may be said to help himself in the child's use of him for help.

Takeo Doi must be credited with bringing the idea of *amae* into clear focus and applying it to a wide range of child and adult phenomena in Japan (and elsewhere) in his two best-known books, *The Anatomy of Dependence* (1971) and *The Anatomy of the Self* (1985). In one's immediate family, argues Doi, even as an adult, it is permissible to *amaeru,* since one may depend upon the helpful sacrifices of family members. One need not restrain oneself nor follow norms of courtesy as one might in less intimate social relationships. One need not worry about imposing upon the other by asking for help, nor apologize for one's inevitable impositions. In the ideal Japanese family, Doi claims, one exists in a state of secure (inter)dependence. One is secure in the knowledge that one's requests for help will be met, and, more importantly, one is secure in the knowledge that one's desires for help will not lead to rejection or the loss of the good will of loved ones.[1]

Here, it is important not to associate help and dependence with mere survival needs, but with the emotional needs that compose the child's primary relationships. As with the concept of help, the concept of *amae* describes not only the orientation of the child toward primary attachment-figures but the web of relatedness in which this dependence occurs. The idea of *amae,* then, is more robust than what attachment theorists would describe as a "secure base" (Bowlby 1988), and more complex than what Freud would call "the child's primary object-choice" (1964, 180). It accords best with what psychoanalytic object-relations theorists refer to as an adaptive and nurturing facilitating en-

---

1 Doi writes that in Japanese society, a useful distinction may be drawn between the inner and outer circles of relationship. According to Doi, when in the inner circle, both the child and the adult are "protected and permitted to *amaeru*" (1971, 107) while, within the other circle, the individual is asked to exercise *kigane* (気兼ね, "restraint"), to refrain from expressing willfulness or personal desires, and to strive primarily for the harmony of the group. To *amaeru* where one ought not is to presume the accommodation of those who do not owe one anything, and is a criticism that has been levied against insufficiently sober individuals and student protest movements alike (see Doi 1971; 1985). Today, to the extent that *hikikomori* is considered a "national" problem with consequences for the entire Japanese nation and economy, this criticism is applied to individuals in *hikikomori* and their families.

vironment (see, e.g., Winnicott 1965). Indeed, the widely held Japanese belief, cited by Doi (1971, 20), that a healthy *jibun* (自分, "self") grows from "the soil" of *amae* in early relationships is quite similar to the Winnicottian notion that the child's capacities for creativity and autonomy are facilitated through satisfactory early experiences of help, facilitation, and dependence.

An adequately helpful environment, from the child's perspective, permits the child to experience dependence as omnipotence and predictability as creativity, while at the same time discovering the roots of secure attachment with parents and an emotional connection with her own authentic impulses and needs. The child who is able to indulge herself in all that is offered her is able to establish the feeling that her external and internal worlds are dependable, worthy, and good. If, however, dependence is no longer available or is unable to be taken advantage of, the result is ontological insecurity: uncertainty about the self's reality (Laing 1969). An ontologically insecure individual lacks "a sense of his presence in the world as a real, alive, whole" and, therefore, lacks "a centrally firm sense of his own and other people's reality and identity […] of the permanency of things, of the reliability of natural processes […] of the substantiality of others" (39).

A child whose need for a helpful (even indulgently helpful) relationship has been unmet inhabits a world quite different from that of the ontologically secure person, for whom "relatedness with others is potentially gratifying." The ontologically insecure person must be "preoccupied with preserving rather than gratifying himself: the ordinary circumstances of living threaten his *low threshold* of security" (Laing 1969, 42, emphasis in original). An individual suffering from losses or deprivations of *amae,* then, contends with a world whose "everyday happenings […] come to have a different hierarchy of significance from that of the ordinary person." The ontologically insecure individual begins to "live in a world of his own' or has already come to do so" (43).

Frustration in the desire for *amae* is a complex phenomenon and is too often blamed squarely on some essential attribute of the child (e.g., his "temperament") or on some obvious failing of the parent. Doi describes a conversation with an extremely anxious patient's mother, who characterized the patient's childhood as one in which the child "did not *amaeru* much (in other words, she kept to herself, never 'made up to' her parents, never behaved childishly in the confident assumption that her parents would help her)" (1971, 18). Such children in Western countries might be described as independent or "easy-going," when, in fact, their lack of assertiveness may reflect an inability to express desires for care and attention.

A relational approach would suggest that frustration in *amae* arises due to a set of unfortunate experiences, fantasies, and fears developed within the parent–child relationship. Specifically, the child who does not *amaeru* may not only fear the experience of frustration of his immediate needs or desires, but, more fundamentally, may fear the negative psychic consequences of expressing or fulfilling them. These consequences may include the shameful perception of his self as greedy, unworthy, or ridiculous, the conscious awareness of his neediness, or the feared rejection or loss of love of the parent.

What is striking about the literature on *hikikomori* is that, in almost every case, the presence of *amae* as a Japanese cultural norm is understood to be a cause of *hikikomori*. Although *amae* is not a new construct, believed instead to have been a part of Japanese culture for centuries (Doi 1971), it is, ostensibly, this same Japanese dynamic that has suddenly generated millions of individuals who find themselves unable to leave their rooms. *Amae,* then, is imagined to be both the very ground from which springs healthy Japanese citizens and an intrusive, culture-wide parenting practice that cripples the child's capacity for independence that is, in spite of all, still "considered adaptive by Japanese standards" (Teo, Stufflebaum, and Kato 2014, 449).

We may wonder why so many studies on *hikikomori* that discuss *amae,* even those that cite Doi's well-known work (see, e.g., Horiguchi 2012; Hein 2009), mistake the construct as an unhealthy parental dependence, while, although dependence likely accompanies an accommodating early childhood environment, a more balanced notion of *amae* would be one in which the child's receipt of loving help were imagined to contribute to a secure attachment and a stable self-relationship. It is tempting, on this point, to speculate that researchers concerned with *amae* are, themselves, articulating a denial of dependence and a denial of their desire for *amae* by pathologizing a healthy aspect of a child's environment. The concomitants of such denials, which include envy and rage, are discussed in greater detail below.

Interestingly enough, this very dynamic is currently being played out in American cultural conversations about its own youth population, particularly the generation known as "post-millennials," or, as Jean Twenge calls them, members of "Generation Me," who are frequently described as uniquely "narcissistic" (Twenge 2006; Twenge and Campbell 2009). Unfortunately, for Twenge and others, "narcissism" has lost its analytic precision and has come to be confused with excessive self-love and self-centeredness derived from the over-indulgence of parents and communities. At the same time, informal diagnoses of American younger generations as lacking "grit" have become increasingly fashionable (see Duckworth et al. 2007).

The calls for "grit" cohere with the accusations of narcissism in that they both claim that today's young people lack the toughness needed to endure an exacting adult world that demands humility, pain, and sacrifice. One wonders, of course, whether the tough, painful, and exacting world held up by these writers as "reality" is not, in fact, a sadistic fantasy in which young people must be made to suffer, perhaps in the same ways that earlier generations have suffered or imagined themselves to have suffered.

What is more, as Heinz Kohut noted, difficulties in school or work, that is, difficulties in mobilizing effort toward defined goals, are not the result of excessive self-esteem but the opposite: "Many of the most severe and chronic work disturbances," Kohut argued, are "due to the fact that the self is poorly cathected with narcissistic libido and in chronic danger of fragmentation."

Since "a relationship to an empathetically approving and accepting parent is one of the preconditions for the original establishment of a firm cathexis of the self" (1971, 120), the individual who has been indulged in *amae* is *less* likely to refuse school, refuse work, or evince other difficulties in pursuing goals than an individual who experienced a frustration of *amae*.

Part of the reason for this is the fact that an appropriate helping (facilitating) environment encourages the development of creative capacities in the child, such that the goals to which study or work may be directed are not foreign, hostile impositions but are (at least partly) self-generated, self-endorsed aims. The difference between these two types of experiences is considerable, and coincides with the differences described above between the ontologically secure and ontologically insecure person. If there is "a living self in depth [that] has become the organizing center of the ego's activities," then the individual's work is "undertaken on his own initiative rather than as if by a passively obedient automaton [… with] some originality rather than being humdrum and routine" (120).

Thus, the misconstrual of *amae* as a pathological self-indulgent and dependent attitude, instilled in the Japanese child, would suggest that the solution to *hikikomori* lies in increased "grit" and toughness, or in the steady deprivation of accommodation and care. At a practical level, this line of thinking has led to the popular belief that "*hikikomori* can be cured with tough love and being kicked out of their nest" (Hairston 2010, 319), and to the development of organizations like the aforementioned "recovery" camps where individuals in *hikikomori* were tormented and, in some cases, even tortured and killed.

On a metaphorical level, this line of thinking threatens the (already threatened) individual in *hikikomori,* and what he represents, with a renewed deprivation of help and care. In maligning *amae* as bad and dangerous desire, and in threatening those who do desire *amae,* much of the extant literature on *hikikomori* expresses envy, rage, and hatred toward individuals in *hikikomori,* who are imagined to greedily presume upon their parents for reliable help in the form of tolerance, shelter, and more. Individuals in *hikikomori,* then, represent a powerful desire for *amae* that must be repressed and disclaimed as a defense against the pain of its frustration. This dynamic of frustrated desire for *amae,* repression or disavowal of this desire, and envy and victimization of those who might possess or fulfill this desire, applies not only to the literature on *hikikomori* but to individuals in *hikikomori,* themselves.

§

If we focus on the individual's desire for *amae,* we see that this desire is not in itself unreasonable, just as the child's desire to be loved, helped, and cared for is healthy and fundamental. But individuals with frustrated desire for *amae,* having internalized a prohibition against experiencing of this desire in order to avoid the pain of failing to fulfill it, must believe it to be shameful and inappropriate, and must recruit others to agree with this belief. By making it appear as if parental love is equivalent to damaging over-indulgence, it is implied not only that the desire is out of place, but that the desire is not even the individual's own. That is, the adult would never have developed this shameful desire had not his culture foolishly encouraged it in his parents. By transforming *amae* into a form of culturally sanctioned parental abuse that facilitates mental suffering as in *hikikomori,* and by implicitly threatening those in *hikikomori* with the "solution" of withdrawing help and care, those concerned with *hikikomori* are able transform their frustrated desires for *amae* into rage against those who seem to receive the help they envy.

If *amae* is imagined to be or to lead to a severe sickness, and if the desire for *amae* is seen as evidence of this sickness, then those who possess this sickness, although quite isolated, are frightening carriers of a dangerous disease. What is feared is not that someone in *hikikomori* may commit a violent or criminal act, but that the truth about *hikikomori* is intolerable because it exposes a repressed desire which cannot be recognized without extreme shame. It is with this metaphor in mind that Franz Kafka's *The Metamorphosis* becomes a relevant narrative to explicate the dynamics of *hikikomori* and its treatment in academic and popular cultures.

In Kafka's well-known story, traveling salesman Gregor Samsa awakens one morning to find that he has been "mysteriously" transformed into an *ungeheuren Ungeziefer*. The term *ungeheuren Ungeziefer* literally means "monstrous vermin" and is translated into English either as such or as "gigantic insect," based upon details given later in the story that suggest Gregor's form to resemble that of a beetle or roach.[2] The Samsa family, including Gregor, does not know exactly what Gregor is, and Kafka himself insisted that no picture of the creature be illustrated anywhere in the publication of the story.

Gregor has changed dramatically, he is no longer recognizable, his speech is no longer human, and his metamorphosis is a mystery. And clearly, Gregor's transformation alters several things about Gregor's life and relationships. What presses most heavily on Gregor's mind at the outset is that Gregor is unable to work and is therefore unable to earn money. Since the collapse of his father's business, Gregor's "sole desire was to do his utmost to help the family [...] so he had set to work with unusual ardor and almost overnight had become a commercial traveler instead of a little clerk" (Kafka 1971, 110). Gregor's tireless work for an abusive chief clerk meant that he was "able to meet the expenses of the whole household" (111). But now, he can no longer be depended upon to provide for his family, whom Gregor has been indulging, in the worst sense, for five long years.

In this time, Gregor's household, and its inhabitants had become rather accustomed to depending upon Gregor's help and self-sacrifice: "They had simply got used to it, both the fam-

---

2   Anyone familiar with Kafka will know that there are countless theories and interpretations of his most famous short story, filling volumes upon volumes of literary criticism. Due to limitations of space, I cannot review this body of critical work here and can advance but one interpretation, not mutually exclusive of many others, which I hope that the reader will find persuasive in its own right and in light of its application to the phenomenon of *hikikomori*.

ily and Gregor; the money was gratefully accepted and gladly given, but there was no special uprush of warm feeling" (111). Moreover, it was admittedly an excessively large household, one that employed a housekeeper and a cook. Gregor's father, in his retirement, had grown "sluggish" and "fat," and Gregor's sister Grete enjoyed "dressing herself nicely, sleeping long […] going out to a few modest entertainments, and above all playing the violin" (112). A portion of Gregor's earnings had even been set aside each month, adding to what was left over from the family business, to develop a small capital sum. These thoughtless spending and saving habits could have been changed to pay off Gregor's father's debts such that Gregor could quit his job, resume something of a normal life, and seek a potential spouse (112).

In one sense, Gregor's transformation sets him free, for Gregor can no longer work. The German word *Verwandlung* can mean not only "metamorphosis" or "transformation" but "commutation," as in the commutation of a punishment or prison sentence. But in another sense, Gregor's freedom and even his very life now depends on the help of his family. Gregor must be fed; his room must be cleaned. To the extent that the family continues to regard the vermin as Gregor, they must nourish and protect him, to see that he is as well as he can be.

Of course, although Gregor is in one sense free and in another sense dependent, Gregor is also *ungeheuer,* monstrously and hideously disfigured. His disfigurement means that he does not appear to be himself (his *false* self), and therefore must be locked away in his room, prevented from interacting with his family in the usual way. Gregor's bedroom is now more like a cage. Gregor, himself, adapts rather quickly to his new "monstrous" condition, as he soon asserts his right to eat what suits his new tastes, defends certain comforts of his room, and, even more than before, protects the symbol (a framed picture of a woman) of his unsatisfied romantic and sexual desires.

So in this story we find a complex set of dynamics similar to those of the individual in *hikikomori*. Gregor indulges his family to such a great extent that he cannot indulge himself in their help nor experience being helped by them. Gregor is unable to *amaeru* to his family, and his narration and behavior strongly suggest that he suffered severe early frustrations and failures in his receipt of love, help, and care. One clue to this state of affairs is Gregor's willingness to take on the burden of the family's obligations, to consider their perspective before his own, and to suffer for their "sins." Gregor neither receives "warm feelings" of gratitude for his labor, nor blames his family for their apparent indifference to his suffering, both prior to and after his transformation. This condition of neglect and abuse at home is recapitulated in Gregor's job, where he is victimized and tormented by a tyrannical boss and an exacting travel schedule to which he must constantly adapt. Another clue comes at the end of the story, when, after Gregor has been dispensed with, the Samsa parents begin to scheme about arranging a lucrative marriage for their daughter, implying that the family will continue to exploit and abuse its children instead of helping and indulging them.

Gregor's physical death is caused by starvation, but Gregor's existence, his self or his psychic existence, is terminated the moment his sister Grete's convinces the family that they "must just try to get rid of the idea that this is Gregor" (134), a notion that she defends by arguing that the real Gregor would be too considerate to presume upon his family's help and sacrifice for so long, and that the real Gregor would have killed himself or removed himself from the home for their sakes long ago in order to help out the family. If we imagine, for a moment, that Gregor has not physically changed at all, we may read his transformation as a metaphor for Gregor's newly found desire to help himself and to be helped. Gregor's desire "monstrously" disfigures him with respect to his own self-concept and his family's impression of him. In a sense, Grete is right that, if all the family knows of Gregor is his willingness to exploit himself in their service, Gregor no longer exists. In the moment of his death, Gregor, tragically, comes to agree with the family that he, in his new "monstrous" form, is not himself and therefore must be eliminated. Kafka writes that, in the end, Gregor thought of his family with tenderness and love. The decision that he must disappear was one that he held to even more strongly than his sister, if that were possible. In this state of vacant and peaceful meditation he remained until the tower clock struck three in the morning… then his head sank to the floor of its own accord and from his nostrils came the last faint flicker of his breath. (135)

Gregor's "mysterious" transformation is, at once, a claim to help and care, a self-degradation, and an escape from a painful condition. What is compelling and tragic about the story, of course, is that it should not be necessary that Gregor be monstrously disfigured in order to access his own desire, to free himself from an unnecessarily abusive situation, and to ask (implicitly) for help. That is, Gregor's transformation may be read as an attempt to rediscover his capacity to *amaeru*. This attempt ultimately fails because Gregor is unable to experience or act upon his desire for *amae* without becoming overwhelmed by shame and self-loathing, disfiguring his desire into something hideous. Gregor both strives to fulfill and sabotages his struggle for *amae* by becoming "monstrous" to those from whom he most deeply desires love.

If it is the internal conflict between Gregor's shame and his desire to *amaeru* that causes his disfigurement and monstrosity, then his metamorphosis appears very much like the metamorphoses of scores of Japanese young men and women who enter *hikikomori,* who feel that their desire for *amae,* expressed in a sort of half-measure of dependent but not indulgent behavior, makes them monstrous and unworthy of *amae*. It would seem that the metamorphosis, as it were, of the socially functioning individual to the individual-in-*hikikomori* is characterized by both profound shame and impossible hope, or, to be more precise, hope made impossible by an equally powerful sense of shame.

Since the individual in *hikikomori* experiences his desire to *amaeru* as childish, shameful, or monstrous, his silent self-incarceration may be understood as a desperate attempt to enter a protective "cocoon" from which he may one day emerge not as a disfigured vermin full of monstrous desires but as a person worthy of help and care. As Winnicott might say, such an individual is attempting to "get back behind the deprivation moment or condition" (1986, 92) to return to a child-like state of freedom, dependence, and help, lost long ago. But the ambivalence about this desire, due to the shame the individual has internalized as a defense against its early failure or frustration, suggests to him that returning to this state is neither possible nor desirable, and therefore tantamount to the loss of his recognizable self and to his own psychic death. The impossibility of his hope, then, turns the individual in *hikikomori* to anger, as he repeats rather than redeems his moment of deprivation while seeking to impose his deprivation onto others. To understand these final characteristics of *hikikomori,* we must conclude with a brief reflection on Winnicott's work on deprivation and delinquency.

§

In his short paper entitled "Delinquency as a Sign of Hope," Winnicott is concerned with children who have experienced deprivation: the loss or withdrawal of help, dependability, or even indulgence in their worlds. Deprivation may be painful in terms of the frustration of momentary needs or desires, but, more importantly, it occasions a tremendous change in the entire psychosocial experience or "the whole life of the child" (1986, 91). That is, deprivation is *not* experienced by the child as a trivial or temporary environmental failure. The child, possessed at first by "unthinkable anxiety" about his new condition (92), quickly strives to comply with the new order of things, fundamentally because "there is nothing else that the child is strong enough to do" (92).

But adaptation to a depriving and impoverished environment means the loss of the child's immature yet authentic self, the loss of the spontaneous child who does not first consider others' perspectives before expressing or acting upon (or becoming aware of) his own needs and desires. Although he had little choice, the child who identifies with the framework of control and deprivation inflicts a greater loss upon himself. He compounds his initial loss — we might even say he unwittingly colludes with his depriving objects and environment — to produce a state of profound self-deprivation.

Nevertheless, as mentioned above, Winnicott posits that it is common for children who can still recall an earlier state of help to seize upon an occasion for hope, and to strive to return to a time antecedent to the deprivation, undoing their current predicament (92). Since the child deprived of an adaptive environment is prevented from creatively finding and using objects, and since the deprived child becomes further identified with others' needs and the rules governing an uncreative and unforgiving environment, the child's initial impulsive acts represent creative seeking more than anti-social delinquency. That is, the child may impulsively steal or break something, but such acts of theft or destructiveness are really an attempt to creatively find objects and to experience the safe expression of aggressiveness (94–95). Ultimately, what the child hopes for in cases of apparently "delinquent" behavior is a return to the state in which the child's spontaneous needs and desires had been indulged and facilitated by the parent. Winnicott recommends, therefore, as an appropriate response to acts of delinquency, "a temporary period of indulgence which may very well see the child through a difficult phase" (94).

The same may be said of individuals in *hikikomori*: that they have suffered from some deprivation, that they are behaving in a way that appears asocial and anti-social, but that ultimately they seek not rebellion nor destruction but to return to a condition of creative living, connection with their own desires (even the childish ones), and, for lack of a better term, "helpful" self-experience. In spite of such hopes, the individual in *hikikomori* compulsively re-enacts his deprivation, attaching a more regressive aim to his behavior: the hope of sharing his deprivation with others by visiting his suffering upon them. Thus, we must consider the aggressive and victimizing components of *hikikomori* along with as the hopeful ones.

The state of self-incarceration and self-deprivation imposed by the individual in *hikikomori* tacitly denies family members the freedom and autonomy due to subjects as separate individuals. But it would be a mistake to imagine that an individual's state of *hikikomori* forces family members to return to *amae.* At least, such an interpretation would seem to offer a very shallow understanding of what *amae* signifies and what is ultimately hoped for. Family members caring for an individual in *hikikomori* are both prevented from emotionally interacting with the individual and relegated to providing the individual with meals, clothing, shelter, and other basic needs. Family members often make tremendous sacrifices in their own lives to take care of the individual in *hikikomori.*

The *refusal to help,* on the part of the individual in *hikikomori,* the family understand the trying situation leaves family members unsure whether the *hikikomori* is a punishment for some misdeed, or whether it will lead to sickness, violence, or suicide. Parents and family members of individuals in *hikikomori* are subjected to social stigma and frequently report feelings of guilt and shame concerning their *hikikomori* family member. Indeed, "in order to avoid criticism and even ostracism, the parents of those with *Hikikomori* hide their shut-in children from their relatives, neighbors, and their communities" (Hattori 2005, 198).

By denying communication, by shutting family members out, and by abandoning family members in their shame, worry, and fear, the individual in *hikikomori* victimizes his family members while similarly occupying the position of a victim. Part of the victimization involved in *hikikomori,* then, is that the individual who is merely shut away in his room manages to deprive others of psychological well-being, comfort, self-esteem, participation in normal activities and relationships, and the ability to help themselves and to receive and enjoy the help of others. The individual in *hikikomori* makes others responsible for his survival and, by implication, for his *hikikomori* state as well.

Gary Paul's very short story, "Hikikomori," shares something of the effect of *hikikomori* on a sibling with a painful simplicity (2012, 69–70). In the story, Satoshi writes a note to his sister to accompany her nightly meal, left outside of her door. Satoshi has not seen her in five years.

> I hope you're still alive and well. I mean, someone eats the plates of food I leave outside your door... I'm just writing this letter because I wanted to talk to you in some way or another... That reminds me, the school still sends me letters asking when you'll be coming back. I don't know how to reply to them. Oh, don't think I'm pressuring you to come out or something. Just want to talk...
>
> As for me, I had a girlfriend last year! You may have heard us talking and laughing loudly late at night. She made me laugh. She wanted to meet you, you know, but... we're not together any more. I couldn't leave the house for too long, not with you left all alone here. I don't mean to sound bitter, I like looking after you. Think I'm a little bit *hikikomori* myself, haha. I don't do much these days. I don't know why... I just feel sort of numb. The world has gotten harder in the last few years. I'm not sure I want to be a part of it any more. Honestly, caring for you is the only thing I think I'm good at, and, even then, I don't know if I'm succeeding...
>
> I love you.
> Happy Birthday.
> — Satoshi

To consider *hikikomori* a means of punishing others by punishing the self, and, as such, as a form of victimization via self-victimization, is to interpret *hikikomori* along the lines of Theodor Reik's understanding of masochistic behavior as symbolic aggression that announces: "That's how I would like to treat you" (see Uebel 2013, 480–81). Indeed, it would not be out of order to speculate that a goal of the individual in *hikikomori* is to transmit to family members and others his own loss, shame, anger, and fear. Doing so permits the individual in *hikikomori* to re-experience his own deprivation and to experience, perhaps for the first time, his confusion and anger by projectively identifying with the family's suffering.

Developmentally speaking, we may say that early deprivation is a kind of victimization, or, to put it another way, the deprivation of help, dependence, or *amae* is the original act of victimization. To be deprived of *amae* is a form of victimization that leads many individuals to carry with them, throughout life, a sense of having been profoundly harmed. In adulthood, individuals and groups continue to make use of the mechanism of projective identification to re-create this early victimization, to experience their own feelings through other's reactions to being victimized, and to impose upon others the responsibility for their own acts of victimization.

Indeed, in politics, this dynamic may be frequently seen, as in the Zenkyōtō student movements in Japan in the 1960s discussed by Doi, who noticed that that both *amae* and *higai-sha-ishiki* (被害者意識, "the sense of grievance and of being a victim") were at work, and that the two constructs were closely connected. Doi remarked how the students of the Zenkyōtō movements were able to operate aggressively while, at the same time framing their actions in ways that succeeded in "putting themselves in the position of victims" (1971, 25–26). More recently, in the United States, the killings of Black men by police officers in Ferguson, Missouri, New York City, and elsewhere, and the unfortunate police responses to public protest and outrage, have shown that police, government, and civilian groups of diverse orientations are all capable of casting themselves as victims and, as such, of acting with the objective of transmitting and re-transmitting their own experiences of suffering, imposing upon others the agony, confusion, and incomprehension of the victim.

That individuals in *hikikomori* remain shut away in their room and seem to refuse, for years and even decades, gestures of help and understanding from family members and social workers, implies that the problem lies not in Japanese culture, but in the tragic repetition of an early failure in the relationship between child and parent, such that the individual in *hikikomori* is now unable to accept his own desire but is also unable to abandon it. The resistance to accepting help by the individual in *hikikomori* is, as suggested above, related to the extreme shame felt by such individuals: the disfiguring of their desire as shameful and monstrous, which only further deepens their sense of shame and unworthiness. The inability to abandon the desire for *amae* is related to unyielding feelings of rage and resentment at having lost the help and care due a child and the subsequent losses suffered by the ontologically insecure adult.

The desire for *amae* is mystified by the individual in *hikikomori,* as it is mystified in the extant literature on *hikikomori*. The individual in *hikikomori* disguises his desire for *amae* by depriving himself of all possibility of loving contact in an endless repetition of his deprivation and its shame and loneliness. Furthermore, while occupying the place of the victim, he victimizes the very people from whom he hopes for loving help and care by enjoining them to provide for him and by inflicting upon these people personal restrictions as well as feelings of fear, guilt, anger, and confusion. The literature on *hikikomori* likewise disavows the desire for *amae* by maintaining that it is the presence of *amae,* rather than its deprivation, that lies at the root of the problem. If the original hope of the individual in *hikikomori* was to return to a state in which his own childish desire for love, help, and care could be expressed and fulfilled without feeling shame, the individual in *hikikomori,* and the literature that purports to treat him, ends by hiding this hope and disfiguring the desire at its core into something monstrous that must always be kept shut away on "the other side of the door."

Trauma and the Self

Trauma is often represented in the psyche in medical terms, like a wound that penetrates the skin or tissue of the body. The standard narrative has become that trauma happens too quickly for the individual to process it, so it sticks, as it were, in the body, in an unconscious psyche-soma, from where it haunts its victims.

But an extraordinary or overwhelming event does not a trauma make. I want to speak about trauma in terms of relationships, to get away from the *event orientation* of trauma. Because many traumas refer back to early relationships and their failures, trauma itself may come to be held in the mind as a means of relating to others, to the world, to the self: a relationship full of anxiety, ambivalence, terror, and hate.

Parents can alleviate and untangle many traumas of childhood if help is given appropriately. The only trauma they cannot help is their own failure of help toward their children, which may be described, then, as a traumatic relationship from which there is no escape.

§

What if we ceased to speak about "traumatic events" altogether? I know that is hard for some to hear — "What about watching a soldier shoot a child in front of you?," etc. It is not that this event is non-traumatic — and why? Because it relates to extremely powerful attachments, meanings, and purposes, and even to our own experiences of helplessness as children, which is very much the point. Only, it would be clearer if we said it was likely to be experienced traumatically.

I wish to draw a distinction that is simple enough between *traumata,* which include specific and limited events, stressors, triggers, and the like, and *traumatic experience,* which is dynamic, relational, and contextual. That is, we cannot speak meaningfully about traumata as trauma because we do not know about the individuals, relationships, or contexts involved. All this is not to say that a "traumatic event" is somehow not as horrific as we imagine it. Trauma is not or should not be a symbol to indicate the highest degree of gravity, impact, horror, or atrocity.

What makes traumata into traumatic experiences is that the traumata recall (re-call/*rappel*) early experiences that were traumatically processed and that left gaps, damage, ruptures, or schisms in the circuital structure of the psyche, such that the traumata fall into one of those ruptures or schisms and make contact with a pre-existing wound.

Here, I cannot help but return to the medical definition of trauma, where, while it may be confusing in some cases, there is a useful metaphor to be found, but only if we imagine that no one emerges from childhood without various psychic wounds, cuts, and bruises, if not much worse. Then, we can imagine how a later event could re-aggravate an old injury. Here, rather than conceiving of the trauma as the injury itself, I conceive of it as a disruption in the self's relation to itself given its pre-existing wounds, best understood adjectivally or even adverbially as *traumatically* encoded or *traumatically* experienced feelings of helplessness, as traumatically blocked or disrupted self-contact and self-communication.

These disruptions and their traumatic consequences arise first from experiences of helplessness that are, in many ways, intrinsic to childhood. As I have argued, even extraordinarily capacious and attuned parents will fail their children, and not all (perhaps not many) parents are extraordinarily capacious and attuned. This helplessness, however, is not anxiety itself, nor is it trauma.

How the experience of helplessness is handled is what leads to anxiety or traumatic experience (or not). Most often, in a state of helplessness, the child feels a combination of terror and hate — and hate of the terror. If the child is of an age where it is appropriate to speak of blame, then it is possible for the child to blame the parent whose failure(s) caused him to feel helpless.

Trauma arises not passively, but when a failure of help is internalized as traumatically encoded shame, as an apparent attack on the self from an individual or group from which help was expected, that was relied upon. But this can go another way, too. Feelings of hate can arise without being engendered by helplessness. Hate can cause helplessness, in the sense that a young child may not know what to do with his feelings of hate, for, say, his mother. He needs and loves his mother but also hates her. What can he do? If he is brave enough, he may go to the mother in an attempt to sort this out and if the mother is "good enough," she may help him find a way to contain and process some of his feelings of hate and return those feelings to him in a more manageable form.

Even still, the child may end up hating the mother for her seemingly super-human or magical ability to turn overwhelmingly toxic feelings (they need not only be hate) into something ingestible or containable by the child. This envy can then return to hate and the child may find that he is stuck between hate that is unattended to and envious hate at those who attend to and help manage his hate (see "Attacks on Help," this volume).

Negative feelings, primary among them hate, but also fault, shame, rage, and grief, have not been contained and processed by the caregiver in such a way as to permit the child to develop what Freud called the "defensive shield" along the self-boundary. Masud Khan later emphasized that the Freudian defensive shield *is* the "mother." That is, the parent or caregiver either helps the developing child find opportunities to develop a psychic apparatus that can contain and process powerfully negative emotions or does not. In the latter case, the individual will be much more likely to experience events traumatically, to mourn traumatically (i.e., to process loss in a way that is problematic, filled with unresolved ambivalence, hatred, and inner conflict), to encounter the world traumatically, to experience major life events traumatically (i.e., to fail to surmount the challenges of a situation without excessive anxiety and ambivalence about help), and more.

Failures of help (or its excess) lead to helplessness. Helplessness is the defining characteristic of anxiety because one's contact with oneself is threatened. Anxiety is the primary affect of traumatically encoded experience. And traumatically encoded experience underlies anxiety.

Does anxiety signal to the individual that he is becoming overwhelmed with hate? Maybe. This may be why panic and anxiety attacks are so often experienced in paranoid ways, because the hatred is cast outward and reflected back upon the self in a projection, as if everyone hated the individual, rather than the reverse. Concomitantly, panic attacks may well be considered *flashbacks,* just as they are, themselves, traumatic experiences, just not visually determined ones, making panic symptoms quite similar to those suffered by persons with PTSD.

The helpless child has no choice but to develop a traumatic split in his self-connection, a split between (a) the part of self in need of help that is hurt, enraged, then abjected as "bad" and unworthy of help (not to mention, excluded from the family and all aspects of the human community organized around help); and (b) the part of self that must help itself, according to whatever contexts, relationships, and structures of meaning are available.

§

Søren Kierkegaard, who may be regarded as an early relational psychoanalyst, opens his famous *The Concept of Anxiety* with a definition of the self that has, unfortunately, been somewhat underappreciated by those seeking to make of psychoanalysis something other than what Jon Mills has called a mere restatement of the obvious, including theoretical insights that can be found in Freud and Freudians as well as object-relations and self-psychological schools of thought.

Kierkegaard writes: "The self is a relation that relates itself to itself or is the relation's relating itself to itself in the relation; the self is not the relation but is the relation's relating itself to itself" (1980, 13).

We must, however, modify this basic definition somewhat to permit of more than a simple relation — for Kierkegaard, the relation that constitutes the self is between "the finite" (*det endelige*) and "the infinite" (*det uendelige*) — as such: "The self is an unbounded *set* of relations between itself and (internal and external) objects that relate themselves to themselves, or is the relations' relating themselves to themselves in their relations; the self is *not* the set of relations, itself, but is the relations' relating themselves to themselves" (see fig. 1).

It is important to add to this picture an insight drawn from D.W. Winnicott. The necessary presence of a core of reality-feeling that composes the "secret self" and its "incommunicado" element, which survive precisely by being isolated from relating and, so, from the potential for contact with objects that might alter or deform them (1965, 187).

This secret self Winnicott deems absolutely crucial for psychological health and genuine subjective emergence, since the alternative, the idea that all of the self may be available to or penetrable by others, would be crushing. The sequestered re-

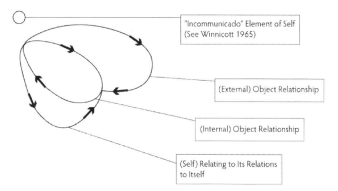

Fig. 1. The self and its circuital structure.

ality-feeling he describes entails a "right not to communicate," derived not from a rational ethical grounding so much as from an inner "protest" that arises in the core of the self against "the frightening fantasy of being infinitely exploited" (179).

At a minimum, two factors are necessary if one is to say that a self is healthy and coherent. It is not enough that the self be related to a set of internal or external objects. Rather, there must be:

1. a high degree of *relatedness* between the self's relations and the self (i.e., the relations are not sealed off from each other or from the self, each one in its own place, *nor* fused together, which would make of them not so much a set of relations as an amalgam of confused, indistinct, and overlapping connections).

2. The self's countless (internal and external) object relations and their relations to the self (see fig. 3) must not impinge upon the self's "right not to communicate," which is to say: There must be room left, amidst all of this relating, for the incommunicado, secret self to remain undisturbed.

The alternative to a healthy, coherent self is a self whose relations between (internal and external) objects and itself are *traumatically constituted,* such that:

1. self–object relations are either unrelated to each other or to the self, where they remain discrete or walled-off, in one case, or tangled, confounded, and overlapping, in the other; or

2. self–object relations are not related to the self in a way that permits of the continued existence of an incommunicado core or secret, secure base of reality-feeling that is free from impingement and the demand to be ready to relate at any moment. If either of these conditions obtain, then self–object–self relations are infused with confusion and conflict, such that there are disruptions, muddles, or breaks where there should be intersections and mutually constitutive relations.

Let us remark upon a few other conclusions that may be drawn from this schema:

3. Internal object relationships mediate external object relationships. To say as much is not to suggest that meaningful and genuine intersubjective relationships are impossible. On the contrary, it is to recognize the mediation of the self's experience in the experience of others. When this mediation is occluded or forgotten (or wished away, as in fantasies of fusion or totalizing experience), a "direct" experience of the other (or the Other) is imagined to be possible. On this point, R.D. Laing's *Politics of Experience* is convincing:

We can see other people's behavior, but not their experience. […] The other person's behavior is an experience of mine. My behavior is an experience of the other. […] I see you, and you see me. I experience you, and you experience me. I see your behavior. You see my behavior. But I do not and never have and never will see your experience of me. Just as you

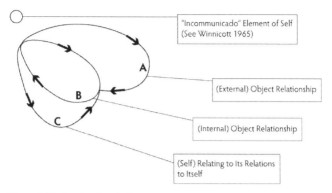

Fig. 2. Self-circuits detailed.

cannot "see" my experience of you. My experience of you is not "inside" me. It is simply you, as I experience you. And I do not experience you as inside me. Similarly, I take it that you do not experience me as inside you [of course, Laing recognizes that we may experience others as 'inside" us, as in infantile fantasy, projective identification, phenomena associated with psychotic functioning, and more]. (1983, 3–4, emphases in original)

What is important in this passage is not the impossibility of genuine empathy or understanding, for that may even become more likely given such considerations, but, rather, put into relational language, the fact that external object relationships are never "pure" or free from internal object relationships, which relationships are almost always multiple, such that multiple internal object relationships inflect relationships even with a single external object or other. For instance, one's relationship with, say, one's priest, or one's teacher, or one's psychoanalyst is mediated and inflected by numerous internal object relationships with, say, one's mother, one's father, ones' former teachers, one's God or object of worship, and more.

An important conclusion to be gleaned from these supposi-
tions is that disruptions in external object relationships may or
may not affect internal object relationships, while the opposite is
not exactly the case. Disruptions to internal object relationships
affect relevant external object relationships, even if the changes
that ensue are not made clear to the other nor made conscious
to the self.

If, for example, there is a disruption at in the external object
relationship (see fig. 2, at point A), it is possible (but not necessary) that the internal object relationship on which lies point
B is altered. For instance, if the internal object relationship between the self and a dying friend is well established, and if various actions, communications, and work is undertaken, then it is
possible for the friend to die and for the internal object relationship to remain (perhaps after a period of grief and mourning)
what it was; that is, to remain more or less intact.

On the other hand, if there is change, disruption, or damage to the internal object relationship then it is impossible that
the external object relationship(s) related with it will remain the
same. This change may be well-hidden, of course, and may be
well-hidden even for noble reasons, say, if one's dying friend is
discovered to have done something that diminishes him in one's
eyes.

One may very well continue on in loving and supporting
one's friend through his final days, but one's experience of him
will be different. If the friend is intuitive and sensitive, he may
well pick up on this change and extend an offer to communicate
about the change, which may go some way toward repairing the
damage in the internal object relationship, or may not, depending on a host of variables too long to list here.

Now consider the circuit on which lies point C, the self's relating its relations to itself. Here, we see that changes in either
external or internal object relationships will affect this relation,
which entails the relations on which lie points A and B. Of
course, the self is engaged in more than one external/internal
object relationship, so we must imagine the self in such a way

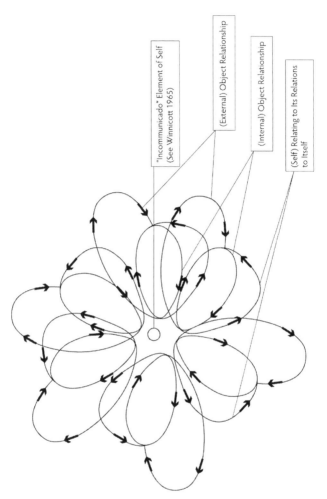

Fig. 3. Self-circuits multiplied.

that it refers to an unbounded set of relations to external objects, internal objects, and to the relations of these to itself.

Because the language of the self's "relating to its relations to itself" can become cumbersome, if not altogether confusing, I have found it helpful to use a different term when describing the connections between self, internal objects, external objects, and reflexive self/object relations.

The term I prefer is an electrical one: *circuit*. Here, it becomes conceptually simpler to imagine overlapping relational circuits which are not, of course, "hard-wired" or inflexible, but are, like electrical circuits, capable of damage, of "overload," of interference with or by other circuits, of being "short-circuited," of being broken, disused, redundant, and more.

Of course, in keeping with the language of the above, the self must not be construed merely as the sum total of these circuits, but, rather, as the incommunicado element of reality-feeling plus the circuital relations of each circuit to itself, to the others, and to the relations between them, themselves.

It is hoped that these brief reflections, combined with a particular approach to trauma may help us to rethink trauma as a disruption of the self's relation to itself, as traumatically endowed or inflected circuitry, allowing us to unite what were formerly disparate schools of thought: the Freudian "overload" and the relational account of trauma and of the self in which trauma is embedded in internal object relationships and external trauma exacerbate those internal deficiencies and disruptions.

Help and Guilt

Albert Camus's novel, *The Fall* (1956), is based on the idea that help is really about vanity or prestige within a social group, rather than any genuine human, ethical, or spiritual calling. It is important that it is called *The Fall* (*La chute*) because the title instantly reminds us of the fall of humankind from the paradise of the Garden of Eden.

Jean-Baptiste Clamence, like Sisyphus and like Camus himself, has a *mal de l'esprit.* He is a "judge-penitent" and former lawyer who specialized in "noble cases" (17), or so he tells an unnamed patron of a bar along the "concentric canals" of Amsterdam, which, Clamence remarks, "resemble the circles of hell" (14).

In his former life as a lawyer, Clamence used to reach the heights of ecstasy when representing those who had been manifestly harmed or abused. "The slightest scent of a victim" set Clamence into swift action.

> And what action! A real tornado! My heart was on my sleeve. You really would have thought that justice slept with me every night. [...] I never charged the poor a fee and never boasted of it. [...] I enjoyed that part of my nature which reacted so appropriately to the widow and orphan that eventually, through exercise, it came to dominate my whole life. For

> instance, I loved to help blind people cross streets. [...] In the same way, I always enjoyed giving directions, [...] obliging with a light, lending a hand to heavy pushcarts, pushing a stranded car, buying a paper from the Salvation Army lass or flowers from the old peddler [...]. I also liked — and this is harder to say — I liked to give alms. [...] I used to exult. (19–21)

All of this, combined with his generous and noble profession, means to Clamence that he was "achieving more than the vulgar ambitious man and rising to that supreme summit where virtue is its own reward" (23)

Clamence's identification with people in need of help is clear, and we know that helping such persons is what satisfies his "conscience," gives him "the feeling of the law, the satisfaction of being right, the joy of self-esteem" (18). These sentiments may give us a clue as to the motivations of helpers, although it would be wrong to infer that all of these, or other motivations, are necessarily as vain or duplicitous as they appear to be in Clamence.

One theme of the story is the brutishness of humanity and the falsehood with which Clamence carried himself, for he would play the part (for an audience) of a lawyer helping a needy victim, but could not bring himself to risk helping a woman who jumped from a bridge. It is ostensibly this failure of help — although we remark the differential of risk involved — that brings Clamence to our attention, but we soon discover there is a deeper moral or religious guilt in Clamence as well.

Clamence, frankly, has a serious problem with guilt; he is, or has, a deeply guilty self. Everything Clamence says and does seems to be about defending against guilt, first by over-compensating with grandiose nobility, then, after his crisis, by confessing it, incessantly talking so as never to "hear" it, trying to "claim" it without really feeling it, and projecting it onto others, onto everyone.

I would argue that even Camus, in writing the book, partakes in and re-enacts this dynamic to a considerable degree.

The book is a self-confessional critique of the vanity of self-confessional critiques, and Camus becomes, in some sense, a "higher-order Clamence" by condemning himself and ensnaring himself (and the reader, perhaps) in his drama of guilt, dragging us all out of the Garden and into "Hell" with him.

As Clamence says, if decent people go around thinking themselves innocent, well, "that's what must be avoided above all. Otherwise, everything would be just a joke" (41). Clamence assuredly does not think himself to be innocent. He knows his nerve has failed him. And yet, he also appears to know that the norms or standards to which he holds himself are falsely heroic. So, does failing to live up to a false standard lead one to the truth? I don't think it does, but Camus seems to think so, and the condemnation of falsehood and duplicity are a very large part of the book.

It is sad to see crows peck empty plastic bags in snow. Crows pecking empty plastic bags in snow are sad. When they caw, I like to think they caw against the snowy and the sad, resolutely against the moment, against the Great Crow, who brings the snowy and the sad, against the situation of themselves against themselves, crow against crow, emptiness upon emptiness, but they don't. That's one difference between us and crows. To watch them from a motel window peck at empty plastic bags in snow makes me want to cry out about the cold and dislocation, the dejection of the scene, its desperation, but crows just caw at plastic bags, without words, without meanings. I do not help them. Until they starve, they'll peck at empty things to see if they are full, never knowing how we, too, have learned to feed ourselves on words, on cries, on nothing, pecking away at empty things to see if they are full.

Duplicity and doubleness are referred to over and over again in Clamence's self-descriptions (as double, two-sided, even Janus-faced) and in religious allusions, such as the fact that Clamence now resides in the heart of Amsterdam which he refers to as the last circle of hell (for Dante, of course, this circle is for traitors against their lords, and is the home of Judas Iscariot).[1]

And isn't that really the dilemma of humanity, expressed in religious terms in the dilemma of Christ, that He is double? Man and god, human and divine? How can one be both, and are we not all both, human and divine, without guilt for not being one or the other? How can one have both parts (and, again, don't we all, even if we just call it our spirit or our intuition of something indescribably precious within?) without one part betraying the other? And which kind of betrayal is worse (see "Sisyphus Doesn't Want Your Help," this volume)?

This guilt expresses a love for ourselves and recognizes that we cannot really live without both and, sometimes, must allow one to step on the other. It is love for the good, the pure, the ideal, and the desire to strive for it, keep it, restore (or repair) it in ourselves and others, but a love that needs to be wary of losing touch with or "betraying" our humanity with all of its own (equally lovable) defectiveness, tendency to err, and wrongdoing.

§

If there were eyes behind the truth, knowing as eyes know, or if there were a face or voice to hear, we would acquiesce and say, "We do not know. We cannot hear." But sans présence, there is no shame in speaking stupidly about the truth, which, not being there, does not care. If a poem could express the truth, it would be long, written by a certain hand, exclaiming in distillations of parsimony the simplest details of life, countless intuitive immutables, such as: "We get used to anything, even the absence of truth." And,

---

1   This circle is also where Ugolino remains. "Ugolino and His Sons" is a set of sculptures by Jean-Baptiste Carpeaux. Count Ugolino conspires against his nephew and then is punished (in life and in Hell) by being locked up with his sons and starved to death. His children, starving, beg him to eat them, out of a filial love that approaches something truly wretched in its extreme pathos.

"Pleasure is less when pleasure is sought." And, "The end is the least important part."

Plato thought the Good contained it. Truth, currency of geometers and gods, dispelled the clouds around the Forms, allowed things to be known. Perhaps a baser truth is Plato's private love, which nearly jumbled Greek philosophy to make a trope of truth for Eros and bliss our highest faculty. Today with the Apostles we say, "The truth shall set us free." But the truth that sets us free is a church to which we tithe our wealth of poverties. It is a truth like a contemplated suicide. If it uncomplicates our disarray, we expect to die with clarity. As for me, I pray for humbler thoughts, only that my truths will reconcile fear and shame enough that I may search for truth again.

It was as if, still dreaming of impossible things, we sat down, one morning, to write. The truth must have squared off against us, like thunder, like drought, like all that was out of our reach, all we feared, all we sought, all whose communion was lost. We could not describe awesome or infinite things, nor shake heavens on our command. We felt the space between God and us was made of, not sealed by, the truth. And yet, we cannot celebrate our fundamental wish with what we have: choices, and slaveries, and hopes, and odd kinds of love.

§

For absurdism to be anything more than comical, it has to have a center of gravity, which is provided by guilt or, as Camus claims in *The Myth of Sisyphus,* by "scorn," a "scorn" sometimes for life, sometimes for the world, sometimes for God, sometimes for all of these, but nevertheless a scorn that animates us, that is imagined to help us recognize, rebel against, and even momentarily surmount our own absurd condition, just as, psychologically, the condemnatory voice becomes momentarily separated from that which it condemns, etc., this scorn is, one might say, the spark or spirit of Dr. Rieux and Tarrou (from Camus's *The Plague*) and Clamence and, really, almost all of Camus's righteously indignant characters. Most of them have a few flaws but are decent enough, and they do decent things, and yet they (still) have profoundly guilty selves.

Clamence verges on the psychotic at those moments when he hallucinates laughter all around him. This laughter is, in some sense, the laughter of God or his angels mocking Clamence, scorning him. Clamence, as far as I can tell, does not really believe in God (whatever that means), but feels very free to throw around religious references. This may be part of his continuing duplicity — again, a major theme of the work and an essential part of guilt; Clamence has guilt over his own duplicity, which he cannot seem to control — his making use of a language and a belief system, and even a deity, in whom he does not believe just to make his public behavior more attractive and interesting. God is now having "the last laugh," as it were.

So guilt and scorn (and self-scorn) are not just parts of Clamence's painful self-discovery (that he is not in Eden, as he once was), but are also his sole connection to the divine, to God. This is, of course, a common version of, but I would argue a dark version of Judeo-Christianity, almost a Kierkegaardian one: that our sin is what connects us to God, that the point of Eden is to show us that Adam's and Eve's direct connection to God puts them outside human history (except not for Kierkegaard) and that we, subsequently, can only be connected to God through Adam's lapse, through sin and penance (Clamence is, once again, a *juge-pénitent* [judge-penitent]). Indeed, even Christ sinned. If he hadn't, he would not have been a person.

Thus, the title, "The Fall," refers to the fall of the unnamed woman on the bridge, to Clamence's own suicide, to the Biblical fall from grace, and to the "modern" fall of humanity into duplicity. One obvious point that has been raised dozens of times about Camus is that he writes as if he were religious because he needs there to be a God as a sort of bad object, someone or something to scorn for permitting human suffering.

§

As a judge-penitent, Clamence no longer engages in his helping profession. And, in his former life, although he did not truly care for the people he served, he certainly seems to have helped many of them. It is the tension, then, between his abundant help and his lack of care (i.e., the fact of his help and the false perception of himself as someone who cares) that has set him on his path.

For Camus, Clamence's words hold some truth because he is right that people do not seem to care about each other enough to make the world a place of true charity and love. At the same time, to condemn himself for helping others with ulterior motivations in mind expresses something of the dilemma of care described above. Because perfect care is an unreachable ideal (not to mention being largely an inward state of mind of the caregiver), there is no amount of care that can make one's help feel genuine, making Clamence's guilt applicable to all who ascribe to this belief. But if help need not derive from care, then the dilemma is eased and we can make and live with our decisions about help — even decisions about risking one's life to help others — with greater clarity and less guilt.

Attacks on Help

Jay Greenberg is correct that Wilfred Bion's famous paper, "Attacks on Linking," represents one of "only a handful of papers that have shifted the centre of gravity of thinking" for psychoanalytic thought and clinical practices (2017, xvii). Its influence, however, is attributable not only to its insight, but to its vagueness, internal contradiction, and seemingly boundless applicability. Because, for Bion, the functions attacked in attacks on linking are not limited or specified beyond "that-which-joins" (1957, 270), today one finds the term used to explain attacks on almost anything, from relating to thought, from experience to emotion, from love to life itself. The result has been a conceptual inflation of "attacks on linking" that devalues its meaning and power.

What is more, Bion never defines the meaning of "links" or "linking," although he does ask that the term draw our attention to "the patient's relationship with a function rather than with the object that subserves a function" (1959, 312). This distinction makes enough sense when Bion speaks about the infant who attacks the maternal breast, whose function is to gratify the infant in a variety of ways. But the analyst's function is not to gratify the adult patient — although this may be the function fantasied by the patient or the analyst. Let us remember at the start that help — albeit less so than care, *caritas,* or love — always risks becoming a linking function that is overly intrusive and diminishing to the recipient.

In both the child and the adult patient, projective identification is the primary mechanism by which attacks on linking are thought to be carried out. In projective identification, qualities or elements of one's internal world are projected onto another, where they are meant to induce the other to embody or behave in accordance with the ejected elements.

If it is the helping function of the analyst that is attacked — a function that includes the potential to help, the capacity to help, the denial of help, and the failure to help — then "attacks on linking" may be more precisely understood as attacks on help via projections that leave the helper helpless. Such attacks, then, include attacks on others' ability to help the recipient, to help other recipients, and to help themselves.

§

Some of Bion's most astute readers, such as Vermote (2017, 78), have correctly criticized Bion's reliance on Kleinian preconceptions, just as Winnicott famously critiqued Klein's decision to ignore "the dependence of the infant on the mother [...] and dig right back in in terms of primitive mechanisms that are personal to the infant" (1989, 448).

Indeed, Bion's Kleinian orientation is perhaps no more apparent than in his elision of the difference between the infant and the adult patient. Throughout his paper, Bion treats the patient and the infant as interchangeable if not identical, using such phrases as "patient or infant" with surprising frequency. He even swaps the two in places where it makes little sense to do so, as in "by the hatred and envy of the *patient* who cannot allow the *mother* to exercise this function" (1959, 314, emphasis added).

To note that infants and patients are not identical is in no way meant to diminish the importance of infantile experience in shaping adult psychic life. Rather, it is necessary to draw the following distinction which we might otherwise be inclined to draw: For the infant, the use of projective identification is required because the infant lacks the mental capacity to relate in any other way, but, for the adult patient, reliance on projective identification signals not a cognitive deficit but his entanglement in a dilemma whereby the "normal" employment of projective identification, having been thwarted in infancy, leads the patient to rely on the "excessive" use of projective identification later in life (Bion 1959, 312). This excessive use of projective identification results from a hatred of thought and reality that originally took hold as a primitive defense in infancy (see also Spillius 2012).

Making this distinction, however, is problematic for Bion, owing to his reliance on Klein, for instance, when he demurs on the matter of what is "normal" and "excessive" and, instead, defers to Klein's (1946) paper, "Notes on Some Schizoid Mechanisms." Furthermore, if one adheres strictly to Bion's line of argument, this distinction becomes untenable, for Bion relies on a Kleinian understanding of a primal envy as a driving force of attacks on linking in both the infant and the adult. Several times in his paper, Bion returns to Klein in this context, perhaps no more directly than when he insists that "the inborn characteristics" of the infant, "namely, primary aggression and envy" (1959, 313), are really at the heart of attacks on linking. Bion's narrative of the etiology of attacks on linking, then, remain inextricably tied to an inborn proclivity to envy.

§

In spite of (and in contradiction to) his reliance on Kleinian envy, Bion claims elsewhere that frustration in communication motivates attacks on linking. On this score, Bion specifically references a patient who claimed that the analyst "could not stand it," where "it" referred to the communication via projective identification attempted by the patient but only partially received by the analyst, who insisted on verbal communication instead (1958, 90–91). The attack carried out by the patient, according to Bion, was an attack on the use of conscious thought and verbal communication to help the patient understand his dilemma.

In "On Arrogance" (1958, 91), Bion describes a similar case in which the analyst's effort to give verbal expression to an encounter seemed to have the effect of "directly attacking the patient's methods of communication." Here, the patient's "link" with the analyst was his ability to employ the mechanism of projective identification. That is, the patient's method of communication was unconscious and "primitive" (92), whereas the analyst offered more conscious and intellectually mature links.

In his paper on "The Differentiation of the Psychotic from the Nonpsychotic Personalities" (1957), Bion turns his attention to internal or intra-psychic links, such as those between "sense impressions and consciousness" (268), between "all that […] leads to consciousness of external and internal reality" and between "thought-processes, themselves" (269). Here, Bion refers to "the formation of symbols," which becomes not so much impossible as infused with terror and strangeness, since the links between the ingredients of symbols or thoughts have been "mutilated." The mental debris that remains seems to surround the patient with what Bion refers to as diffuse, fragmented particles and "minute links," which then become "impregnated with cruelty" and are attached to the "bizarre objects" that now fill up the patient's psychic landscape (269–72).

It is impossible not to notice Bion's emphasis on the substances that make up the patient's psychic landscape having been transformed into minute "particles," which "rid [the patient] of awareness of reality." The image one is left with is that of a shattered or *destroyed inner world.* The cruel objects and "menacing presence[s]" imprisoning the individual "in the [psychotic] state of mind he has achieved" (269) are precisely what are projected onto the analyst, in order that he will come to share the patient's psychotic state of mind.

§

Bion further confuses the matter by claiming at several points that "curiosity" sponsors the patient's attempt to explore intolerable feelings via projective identification. "Curiosity" is quite difficult if not impossible to disentangle from thought, or, in Bion's terminology, alpha function. And it is important to note, but, unfortunately, too complex a matter to consider at length here, the central place Bion affords to curiosity in his papers that treat attacks on linking and his later theory of knowledge, also referred to as "K" (see Bion 1963, 46n1; 1965, 67; Fisher 2011, 46–54).

Bion does not elaborate on the meaning of "curiosity" in relation to attacks on linking, nor does he explicitly derive it from Klein's epistemophilic instinct. So we are forced to ask what, exactly, might be the nature of this curiosity? And what might be its object? Again, in virtually all of Bion's discussions of attacks on linking, it is not curiosity but envy at the parent's ability to contain, moderate, and transform the infant's split-off feelings that plays the central role.

Moreover, it is difficult to understand how curiosity could hold meaning for an infant whose experiences are largely governed by drive-, need-, and want-gratification and the dynamics of the Kleinian paranoid-schizoid position. Beyond its most primitive form, curiosity requires a certain degree of maturity in self- or ego-development, that degree associated with the possibility of being or becoming a self. In this way, it stands in uncomfortable relation to the psychic world of the Kleinian infant, who has no concept of self. Curiosity entails the idea of discovering difference, considering the possibility of what is not present or given. Curiosity is inextricably related to "the self as potential," the expression of the search for "a way to exist as a self," which means "what [...] curiosity seeks to discover, the self seeks to create" (Levine 2011, 37–38), and, as such, stands in uncomfortable relation to both Bion's and Klein's thought.

§

As mentioned above, Bion argues that the "seriousness of these attacks [on linking]" is exacerbated by the mother who refuses "to serve as a repository for the infant's feelings" (1959, 314). An ameliorating factor, on the contrary, is "the mother [who] can introject the infant's feelings and remain balanced" (313). If the infant experiences the mother to be receptive, his evacuated feelings are introjected, then modified and re-presented in manageable ways.

But ultimately, in both cases, envy rears its head. If projected feelings are "den[ied] ingress" into the mother's psyche, it is likely because doing otherwise would make her "prey to the anxiety which result[s] from introjection" of the intolerable feelings (313). In this way, refusals to contain and transform projected feelings are ways of staying sane in the face of potentially psychotogenic elements. On the other hand, if the mother receives and digests the projective identification but "remain[s] balanced" and enjoys a "comfortable state of mind" (313), this very same receptiveness and capaciousness becomes the object of envious and destructive attacks (see also Riesenberg-Malcolm 2001).

In either case, envy seeks to incapacitate the mother figure by attacking her "peace of mind" (Bion 1959, 313). The real catalyst for the attack on linking is envy directed at the (m)other who, whether by deflection or by containment, proffers help by taking in intolerable emotions.

As we have discussed, Bion's Kleinian orientation, among other factors, suggests that envy, and not frustrated communication or curiosity, is really the force driving attacks on linking. Envy, for Klein, is irreducible — or, if reducible, only reducible to the death instinct — and is experienced in relation both to the good and the bad, but particularly to the good. What may be said is that envy is triggered when another possesses something good, something of value. Envy is a destructive impulse to ruin, spoil, or otherwise befoul the good object. It serves, among other aims, to decrease or eliminate gratitude toward the good object that offers gratification or help.

Since Bion asks that we think of the *functions* of objects and not the objects themselves, because of its substantial connections with early help and attachment discussed below, the most reasonable function subserved by the object of the analyst is the function of helping. Whether help is offered or denied, and whether it is successful or unsuccessful, inherent in helping is the idea that the helper is, or contains, something good and valuable. By offering help, apparently without being drawn into the situation of the recipient of help, the act of helping also implies an assertion of an enviable strength and safety not possessed by the recipient. As we know, in literatures on helping, these factors are thought to contribute to the establishment of a "hierarchical relation" with considerable psychological consequences for both helper and helpee (Nadler 2020, 13). Such consequences include subjection to shame, inferiority, domination, and even "symbolic violence" (14).

§

Whether expressed via the work of a group or not, attacks on linking are attacks on the idea that what connects the self to others is help. Since, developmentally speaking, it is true that help is what connects the self to others, attacks on linking may be considered attacks on the reality of attachment and dependency. Owing to its connection with experiences of helplessness, desolation, inferiority, and shame, it would seem that the "help-that-joins" triggers an envy and a rage powerful enough to dismantle efforts to think, act, and relate with others, regardless of whether the helping function is manifest or hidden.

Laisser se Casser

The key, when things are broken, which is not *all the time,* is letting things be broken, unfixed, letting them be messy. The question is how we respond to the mess.

We can accept it, act on it, seek help, let it drive us to despair, or erase it from our consciousnesses.

Whatever the action, the key is to avoid covering up the real meaning of what is broken, letting *that* mess remain at least until we can find it, and face it.

Then, whether we do nothing or something, we avoid the fatal masquerade from which we can never ever desist, not even before ourselves, lest we face the real broken things, there, hiding.

Many people confuse seeking help with breaking the surface of broken things, letting what is lying beneath arise. They do not want help. They do not want to be unbroken. They are paradoxically attached to a helpless condition.

Summa

Help help help. It is a contemplation. Is help the primordial barbaric yawp. Over the roofs of the world. Is help far and wide
high and low over and over the whole world over. We need help
the whole world over. Or change. Yet we call for help in loss
and change. Imagine all we could change. Imagine all. Spare us
loss in times of loss which are perennial like common sage. Real
pressure means we cannot change mixed up with care. Who
cares. Who cares does not help necessarily. Necessarily it is not
that those who care help. Mixed up with care that makes us love.
That makes us one. That makes ours and another's one in the
unimaginative imagination. Perennially makes one out of what
was not. Maybe spare us care and give us common help. Make
us sage over the roofs of the world. Perennially we call help and
someone helps or not as spare as base as basic as spare change
but that is not all.

References

Acker, Kathy. 1978. *Blood and Guts in High School: A Novel.*
New York: Grove Press.

Ainsworth, Mary D. Salter, Mary C. Blehar, Everett Waters, and
Sally S. Wall. 1978. *Patterns of Attachment: A Psychological
Study of the Strange Situation.* New York: Lawrence
Erlbaum.

Allison, Anne. 2013. *Precarious Japan.* Durham: Duke
University Press.

Apter, Emily. 1997. "Out of Character: Camus's French Algerian
Subjects." *Modern Language Notes* 112, no. 4: 499–516.
https://www.jstor.org/stable/3251325.

Arendt, Hannah. 1996. *Love and Saint Augustine.* Chicago:
University of Chicago Press.

Armatinstein, Sherry. 2021. "Six Tips to Overcoming Anxiety
and Phobias." *Psycom,* November 8. https://www.psycom.
net/facing-your-fear.

Aronfreed, Justin. 1968. "Aversive Control of Socialization."
Nebraska Symposium on Motivation 16: 271–320.

Batson, C. Daniel. 2011. *Altruism in Humans.* Oxford: Oxford
University Press.

Bion, Wilfred R. 1957. "Differentiation of the Psychotic from
the Non-Psychotic Personalities." *International Journal of
Psychoanalysis* 38: 266–75. PMID: 13438602.

————. 1958. "On Arrogance." In *Second Thoughts: Selected Papers on Psycho-Analysis,* 86–92. London: Karnac.

————. 1959. "Attacks on Linking." *International Journal of Psychoanalysis* 40: 308–15. Reprinted in *The Psychoanalytic Quarterly* 82, no. 2 (2013): 285–300. DOI: 10.1002/j.2167-4086.2013.00029.x.

————. 1963. *Elements of Psycho-Analysis.* London: Heinemann.

————. 1965. *Transformations.* London: Karnac.

Bowker, Julie C., Matthew H. Bowker, Jonathan B. Santo, Adesola Adebusola Ojo, Rebecca G. Etkin, and Radhi Raja. 2019. "Severe Social Withdrawal: Cultural Variation in Past Hikikomori Experiences of University Students in Nigeria, Singapore, and the United States." *Journal of Genetic Psychology* 180, nos. 4–5: 217–30. DOI: 10.1080/00221325.2019.1633618.

Bowker, Matthew H. 2011. "The Meaning of Absurd Protest: The Book of Job, Albert Camus, and C. Fred Alford's *After the Holocaust.*" *Journal of Psychosocial Studies* 5, no. 2: 163–83. https://www.psychosocial-studies-association.org/wp-content/uploads/2017/01/meaningofabsurbprotest.pdf.

————. 2013. *Albert Camus and the Political Philosophy of the Absurd: Ambivalence, Resistance, and Creativity.* Lanham: Rowman and Littlefield.

————. 2014. *Rethinking the Politics of Absurdity: Albert Camus, Postmodernity, and the Survival of Innocence.* New York: Routledge.

————. 2016. *Ideologies of Experience: Trauma, Failure, Deprivation, and the Abandonment of the Self.* New York: Routledge.

————. 2018. "Analytic and Political Neutrality: Change, Privilege, and Responsibility." *Free Associations* 71: 1–17. DOI: 10.1234/fa.v0i71.194.

————. 2019a. "Activity, Speech, and Change: Progressive Politics and Regressive Fantasies." *Psychoanalysis, Culture & Society* 24: 105–17. DOI: 10.1057/s41282-019-00119-7.

———. 2019b. "Camus and Psychoanalysis." In *Brill's Companion to Camus: Camus Among the Philosophers,* edited by Matthew Sharpe, Maciej Kałuża, and Peter Francev, 305–26. Leiden: Brill. DOI: 10.1163/9789004419247_016.

Bowker, Matthew H., and David P. Levine. 2018. *A Dangerous Place to Be: Identity, Conflict and Trauma in Higher Education.* New York: Routledge.

Bowlby, John. 1969. *Attachment and Loss, Vol. 1: Attachment.* New York: Basic Books.

———. 1988. *A Secure Base: Parent–Child Attachment and Healthy Human Development.* New York: Basic Books.

Brée, Germaine. 1964. *Camus.* Revised First Harbinger Books Edition. New Brunswick: Rutgers University Press.

Brehm, Jack W. 1989. "Psychological Reactance: Theory and Applications." *Advances in Consumer Research* 16: 72–75. https://www.acrwebsite.org/volumes/6883/volumes/v16/NA-16.

Butler, Judith. 2004. *Precarious Life: The Powers of Mourning and Violence.* Verso: London.

Campbell, Lyle. 1998. *Historical Linguistics: An Introduction.* Second Edition. Cambridge: MIT Press.

Camus, Albert. 1956. *The Fall.* Translated by J. O'Brien. First Vintage International Edition. New York: Vintage

———. 1991a. *Between Hell and Reason: Essays from the Resistance Newspaper Combat, 1944–1947.* Edited and translated by Alexandre de Gramont. Hanover: Wesleyan University Press.

———. 1991b. *The Myth of Sisyphus and Other Essays.* Translated by Justin O'Brien. First Vintage International Edition. New York: Vintage.

———. 1995. *The First Man.* Translated by David Hapgood. New York: Knopf.

Carroll, David 1997. "Camus's Algeria: Birthrights, Colonial Injustice, and the Fiction of a French-Algerian People."

Modern Language Notes 112, no. 4: 517–49. https://www.jstor.
org/stable/3251326.

Coates, Dan, Gary J. Renzaglia, and Marlowe C. Embree.
1983. "When Helping Backfires: Help and Helplessness."
In *New Directions in Helping, Vol. 1: Recipient Reactions to
Aid,* edited by Jeffrey D. Fisher, Arie Nadler, and Bella M.
DePaulo, 251–79. New York: Academic Press.

Coles, Romand. 1997. *Rethinking Generosity: Critical Theory
and the Politics of Caritas.* Ithaca: Cornell University Press.

Covington, Coline. 2021. *For Goodness Sake: Bravery,
Patriotism and Identity.* London: Phoenix.

Day, Stacey R. 2012. *Caritas and the Psychospiritual Way: Essays
on Ethics and the Human Estate.* Praha: Nakladatelství
Trigon-Khiny.

de Sousa, Ronnie. 2021. "Forget Morality." *Aeon.* June 23.
https://aeon.co/essays/five-reasons-why-moral-philosophy-
is-distracting-and-harmful.

Derrida, Jacques. 1989. *Memoires for Paul De Man: The Wellek
Library Lectures at the University of California, Irvine.* New
York: Columbia University Press.

———. 1992. *Given Time, I: Counterfeit Money.* Translated by
Peggy Kamuf. Chicago: University of Chicago Press.

———. 2001. *The Work of Mourning: Jacques Derrida.* Edited
by Pascale-Anne Breault and Michael Naas. Chicago:
University of Chicago Press.

Doi, Takeo. 1971. *The Anatomy of Dependence.* Translated by
John Bester. Tokyo: Kodansha International.

———. 1985. *The Anatomy of the Self: The Individual Versus
Society.* Translated by Mark A. Harbison. Tokyo: Kodansha
International.

Duckworth, Angela L., Christopher Peterson, Michael D.
Matthews, and Dennis R. Kelly. 2007. "Grit: Perseverance
and Passion for Long-Term Goals." *Journal of Personality
and Social Psychology* 92, no. 6: 1087–101. DOI: 10.1037/0022-
3514.92.6.1087.

Dumbach, Annette, and Jud Newborn. 2006. *Sophie Scholl and
the White Rose.* Oxford: Oneworld.

Eagleton, Terry. 2000. *The Idea of Culture*. Oxford: Wiley-
Blackwell.

Edwards, Mark W. 2002. *Sound, Sense, and Rhythm: Listening
to Greek and Latin Poetry*. Princeton: Princeton University
Press.

Finkielkraut, Alain. 1987. *La défaite de la pensée* [*The Defeat of
Thought*]. Paris: Gallimard.

Fisher, James V. 2011. "The Emotional Experience of K." In
Bion Today, edited by Chris Mawson, 43–63. New York:
Routledge. DOI: 10.4324/9781315787299-11.

Fisher, Jeffrey D., Arie Nadler, and Bella M. DePaulo, eds. 1983.
New Directions in Helping, Vol. I: Recipient Reactions to Aid.
New York: Academic Press.

Fletcher, Joseph F. 1967. *Moral Responsibility: Situation Ethics at
Work*. Philadelphia: Westminster.

Freud, Sigmund. 1957. "Mourning and Melancholia." In *The
Standard Edition of the Complete Psychological Works of
Sigmund Freud, Vol. 14: On the History of the Psychoanalytic
Movement, Papers on Metapsychology, and Other Works*,
edited and translated by James Strachey with Anna Freud,
237-58. London: Hogarth.

———. 1959. "Inhibitions, Symptoms, and Anxiety." In *The
Standard Edition of the Complete Psychological Works of
Sigmund Freud, Vol. 20: The Question of Lay Analysis and
Other Works*, edited and translated by James Strachey with
Anna Freud, 75–174, London: Hogarth.

———. 1964. "On the Universal Tendency to Debasement in
the Sphere of Love." In *The Standard Edition of the Complete
Psychological Works of Sigmund Freud, Vol. 11: Five Lectures
on Psychoanalysis, Leonardo DaVinci, and Other Works*,
edited and translated by James Strachey with Anna Freud,
179-90. London: Hogarth.

Gergen, Kenneth, and Mary Gergen. 1974. "Understanding
Foreign Assistance through Public Opinion." In *Yearbook
of World Affairs, Vol. 28*, edited by George W. Keeton and
Georg Schwarzenberger, 125–40. London: Stevens and Sons.

————. 1983. "Social Construction of Helping Relationships."
In *New Directions in Helping, Volume I: Recipient Reactions
to Aid,* edited by Jeffrey D. Fisher, Arie Nadler, and Bella M.
DePaulo, 144–66. New York: Academic Press.

Gilligan, Carol. 1982. In *A Different Voice: Psychological Theory
and Women's Development.* Cambridge: Harvard University
Press.

Graves, Robert. 1955. *The Greek Myths.* Baltimore: Penguin.

Greenberg, Jay. 2017. "Foreword." In *Attacks on Linking
Revisited: A New Look at Bion's Classic Work,* edited by
Catalina Bronstein and Edna O'Shaughnessy, xvii–xxii.
London, Karnac.

Greenberg, Jerald. 1980. "Attentional Focus and Locus
of Performance Causality as Determinants of Equity
Behavior." *Journal of Personality and Social Psychology* 38,
no. 4: 579–85. DOI: 10.1037/0022-3514.38.4.579.

Griffin, Miriam T. 2013. *Seneca on Society: A Guide to De
Beneficiis.* Oxford: Oxford University Press.

Guthrie, Ramon. 1968. *Absestos Phoenix.* New York: Funk and
Wagnalls.

Hairston, Marc. 2010. "A Cocoon with a View: Hikikomori,
Otaku, and Welcome to the NHK." *Mechademia* 5: 311–23.
DOI: 10.2307/41510970.

Hanley, Ryan Patrick. 2009. *Adam Smith and the Character of
Virtue.* Cambridge: Cambridge University Press.

Hatfield, Elaine, and Susan Sprecher. 1983. "Equity Theory and
Recipient Reactions to Aid." In *New Directions in Helping,
Volume I: Recipient Reactions to Aid,* edited by Jeffrey D.
Fisher, Arie Nadler, and Bella M. DePaulo, 113–43. New
York: Academic Press.

Hattori, Yuichi. 2005. "Social Withdrawal in Japanese Youth:
A Case Study of Thirty-Five Hikikomori Clients." *Journal
of Trauma Practice* 4, nos. 3–4: 181–201. DOI: 10.1300/
J189v04n03_01.

Heidegger, Martin. 1962. *Being and Time.* Translated by John Macquarie and Edward Robinson. New York: Harper and Row.

Heider, Fritz. 1958. *The Psychology of Interpersonal Relations.* Hoboken: Wiley.

Hein, Patrick. 2009. *How the Japanese Became Foreign to Themselves: The Impact of Globalization on the Private and Public Spheres in Japan.* New Brunswick: Transaction Publishers.

Held, Virginia. 1983. *Feminist Morality: Transforming Culture, Society, and Politics.* Chicago: University of Chicago Press.

Horiguchi, Sachiko. 2012. "*Hikikomori*: How Private Isolation Caught the Public Eye." In *A Sociology of Japanese Youth: From Returnees to NEETs,* edited by Roger Goodman, Yuki Imoto, and Tuukka Toivonen, 122–38. New York: Routledge.

Horney, Karen. 1937. *The Neurotic Personality of Our Time.* New York: Norton.

James, John Angell. 1829. *Christian Charity Explained.* New York: J. Leavitt.

James, William. 1911. *The Varieties of Religious Experience: A Study in Human Nature.* New York: Longmans, Green, and Co.

Jones, Maggie. 2006. "Shutting Themselves In." *The New York Times Magazine.* January 15. http://www.nytimes.com/2006/01/15/magazine/15japanese.html.

K-Web. 2018. "Hypsipylé, Queen of Lemnos." October 6. https://kddsnap.com/greek-myths/hypsipyle/hypsipyle-queen-of-lemnos/.

Kafka, Franz. 1971. "The Metamorphosis." In *The Complete Stories,* edited by Nahum N. Glatzer, translated by Willa Muir and Edwin Muir, 89–139. New York: Schocken Books.

Kagan, Richard, and Shirley Schlosberg. 1989. *Families in Perpetual Crisis.* New York: Norton.

Kato, Takahiro A., et al. 2011. "Introducing the Concept of Modern Depression in Japan: An International Case Vignette Survey." *Journal of Affective Disorders* 135, nos. 1–3: 66–76. DOI: 10.1016/j.jad.2011.06.030.

————. 2012. "Does the 'Hikikomori' Syndrome of Social Withdrawal Exist Outside Japan? A Preliminary International Investigation." *Social Psychiatry and Psychiatric Epidemiology* 47, no. 7: 1061–75. DOI: 10.1007/s00127-011-0411-7.

Keltner, Dacher, Aleksandr Kogan, Paul K. Piff, and Sarina R. Saturn. 2014. "The Sociocultural Appraisals, Values, and Emotions (SAVE) Framework of Prosociality: Core Processes from Gene to Meme." *Annual Review of Psychology* 65, no. 1: 425–60. DOI: 10.1146/annurev-psych-010213-115054.

Kierkegaard, Søren. 1980. *The Concept of Anxiety.* Edited and translated by Reider Thompte with Albert B. Anderson. Princeton: Princeton University Press.

Kitayama, O., T. Saitō, T. Watanabe, and S. Muto. 2001. "Zadankai Hikikomori Ni Tsuite [Hikikomori Forum]." In *Hikikomori [Gendai No Esprit,* Vol. 403], edited by T. Watanabe and S. Muto, 5–34. Tokyo: Shibundo.

Klein, Melanie. 1946. "Notes on Some Schizoid Mechanisms." *International Journal of Psycho-Analysis* 27: 99–110. PMID: 22700275

Kohut, Heinz. 1971. *The Analysis of the Self: A Systematic Approach to the Psychoanalytic Treatment of Narcissistic Personality Disorders.* Chicago: University of Chicago Press.

Kondo, Naoji, Motohiro Sakai, Yasukazu Kuroda, Yoshikazu Kiyota, Yuji Kitabata, and Mie Kurosawa. 2011. "General Condition of Hikikomori (Prolonged Social Withdrawal) in Japan: Psychiatric Diagnosis and Outcome in Mental Health Welfare Centres." *International Journal of Social Psychiatry* 59, no. 1: 79–86. DOI: 10.1177/0020764011423611.

Kosiński, Jerzy. 1976. *The Painted Bird.* Second Edition. New York: Grove Press.

Kristeva, Julia. 1989. *Black Sun: Depression and Melancholia.* Translated by Léon S. Roudiez. New York: Columbia University Press.

Krystal, Henry. 1995. "Trauma and Aging: A Thirty-Year Follow-up." In *Trauma: Explorations in Memory,* edited by Cathy Caruth, 76–99. Baltimore: Johns Hopkins University Press.

Kuhn, Thomas. 1962. *The Structure of Scientific Revolutions.* Chicago: University of Chicago Press.

Laing, R.D. 1961. *Self and Others.* New York: Pantheon.

———. 1969. *The Divided Self: An Existential Study in Sanity and Madness.* London: Penguin Books.

———. 1983. *The Politics of Experience.* New York: Pantheon.

———. 1985. "Mystification, Confusion and Conflict." In *Intensive Family Therapy,* edited by Ivan Boszormenyi-Nagy and James L. Framo, 343–64. New York: Harper and Row.

Laing, R.D., and Aaron Esterson. 1964. *Sanity, Madness and the Family.* New York: Basic Books

Lanzmann, Claude. 1995. "The Obscenity of Understanding: An Evening with Claude Lanzmann." In T*rauma: Explorations in Memory,* edited by Cathy Caruth, 200–220. Baltimore: Johns Hopkins University Press.

Larkin, Philip. 2011 "Aubade." *The Poetry Foundation.* https://www.poetryfoundation.org/poems/48422/ aubade-56d229a6e2f07.

Laub, Dori. 2012. "Traumatic Shutdown of Narrative and Symbolization: A Death Instinct Derivative?" In *Lost in Transmission: Studies in Trauma across Generations,* edited by G. Fromm, 31–54. London: Karnac. DOI: 10.4324/9780429476884-4.

Lee, Francis Wing-lin, ed. 2009. *Initiatives with Youth-at-risk in Hong Kong.* Hong Kong: City University of Hong Kong Press.

Levi, Primo. 1996. *Survival in Auschwitz: The Nazi Assault on Humanity.* Translated by Stuart Woolf. New York: Touchstone.

Levine, D. 2003. *The Living Dead and the End of Hope: An Essay on the Pursuit of Unhappiness.* Denver: Broken Tree Press.

———. 2011. *The Capacity for Civic Engagement: Public and Private Worlds of the Self.* New York: Palgrave.

Levine, David P., and Matthew H. Bowker. 2019. *The Destroyed World and the Guilty Self: A Psychoanalytic Study of Culture and Politics.* London: Phoenix Publishing.

Lewin, Roger A., and Clarence Schulz. 1992. *Losing and Fusing: Borderline Transitional Object and Self Relations.* Northvale: Jason Aronson.

Mackenzie, Compton. 1962. *Certain Aspects of Moral Courage.* New York: Doubleday.

Maner, Jon K., Carol L. Luce, Steven L. Neuberg, Robert B. Cialdini, Stephanie Brown, and Brad J. Sagarin. 2002. "The Effects of Perspective Taking on Motivations for Helping: Still No Evidence for Altruism." *Personality and Social Psychology Bulletin* 28, no. 11: 1601–10. DOI: 10.1177/014616702237586.

Marris, Peter. 1986. *Loss and Change.* Revised Edition. London: Routledge and Kegan Paul.

May, Rollo. 1950. *The Meaning of Anxiety.* New York: Ronald Press.

Mayeroff, Milton. 1971. *On Caring.* New York: Harper & Row.

Murakami, Ryu. 2000. "Japan's Lost Generation: In a World Filled with Virtual Reality, the Country's Youth Can't Deal with the Real Thing." *Time Asia.* Nov. 8. http://edition.cnn.com/ASIANOW/time/magazine/2000/0501/japan.essaymurakami.html.

Nadler, Arie. 2000. *Social Psychology of Helping Relations: Solidarity and Hierarchy.* Hoboken: Wiley.

Nagata, Toshihiko, Hisashi Yamada, Alan R. Teo, Chiho Yoshimura, Takenori Nakajima, and Irene van Vliet. 2011. "Comorbid Social Withdrawal (*Hikikomori*) in Outpatients with Social Anxiety Disorder: Clinical Characteristics and Treatment Response in a Case Series." *International Journal of Social Psychiatry* 59, no. 1: 73–78. DOI: 10.1177/0020764011423184.

Neiman, Susan. 2002. *Evil in Modern Thought: An Alternative History of Philosophy.* Princeton: Princeton University Press.

Noddings, Nel. 1984. *Caring: A Feminine Approach to Ethics and Moral Education.* Berkeley: University of California Press.

Nygren, Anders. 1953. *Agape and Eros.* Translated by P. Watson. London: SPCK.

O'Loughlin, Michael. 2001. "The Development of Subjectivity in Young Children: Theoretical and Pedagogical Considerations." *Contemporary Issues in Early Childhood* 2, no. 1: 49–65. DOI: 10.2304/ciec.2001.2.1.8.

Ohashi, Noriko. 2008. "Exploring the Psychic Roots of Hikikomori in Japan." PhD Dissertation. Pacifica Graduate Institute.

Oliner, Samuel P., and Pearl M. Oliner. 1988. *The Altruistic Personality: Rescuers of Jews in Nazi Europe.* New York: Free Press.

Paul, Gary. 2012. *I Don't Think the Moon Is Real: Collected Flash Fiction from the Wordsmith Challenge.* Raleigh: Lulu.

Peterson, Christopher, and Martin E. Seligman. 2004. *Character Strengths and Virtues: A Handbook and Classification.* Washington, DC and Oxford: American Psychological Association and Oxford University Press.

Rees, Phil. 2002. "Hikikomori Violence." *BBC News.* October 18. http://news.bbc.co.uk/2/hi/programmes/correspondent/2336883.stm.

Riesenberg-Malcolm, Ruth. 2001. "Bion's Theory of Containment." In *Kleinian Theory: A Contemporary Perspective,* edited by Catalina Bronstein, 165–80. London: Wiley.

Said, Edward. 1979. *Orientalism.* New York: Vintage Books.

Saitō, Tamaki. 1998. *Shakaiteki hikikomori: Owaranai shishunki [Societal Hikikomori: A Never-ending Adolescence].* Japan: PHP-Kenkyujo.

——— 2002. *Hikikomori Kyusyutsu Manyuaru [Hikikomori Rescue Manual].* Japan: PHP-Kenkyujo.

Sakamoto, Noriyuki, Rodger G. Martin, Hiroaki Kumano, Tomifusa Kuboki, and Samir Al-Adawi. 2005. "Hikikomori, Is It a Culture-reactive or Culture-bound Syndrome?

Nidotherapy and a Clinical Vignette from Oman." *International Journal of Psychiatry in Medicine* 35, no. 2: 191–98. DOI: 10.2190/7WEQ-216D-TVNH-PQJ1.

Scarre, Geoffrey. 2010. *On Courage.* New York: Routledge.

Scheler, Max. 1961. *Ressentiment*. New York: Free Press.

Scorza, Jason A. 2001. "The Ambivalence of Political Courage." *The Review of Politics* 63, no. 4: 637–62. https://www.jstor.org/stable/1408854.

Shay, Jonathan. 1995. *Achilles in Vietnam: Combat Trauma and the Undoing of Character*. New York: Simon & Schuster.

Shengold, Leonard. 1989. *Soul Murder: The Effects of Childhood Abuse and Deprivation.* New York: Fawcett Columbine.

Shklar, Judith. 1989. "The Liberalism of Fear." In *Liberalism and the Moral Life,* edited by Nancy L. Rosenblum, 21–38. Cambridge: Harvard University Press.

Smith, Kyle D., John P. Keating, and Ezra Stotland. 1989. "Altrusim Reconsidered: The Effect of Denying Feedback on a Victim's Status to Empathic Witnesses." *Journal of Personality and Social Psychology* 57, no. 4: 641–50. DOI: 10.1037/0022-3514.57.4.641.

Spillius, Elizabeth. 2012. "Developments by British Kleinian Analysts." In *Projective Identification: The Fate of a Concept,* edited by Elizabeth Spillius and Edna O'Shaughnessy, 49–60. London: The New Library of Psychoanalysis.

Staub, Ervin. 1979. *Positive Social Behavior and Morality, Vol. 2: Socialization and Development.* New York: Academic Press.

Stevens, Wallace. 1951. *The Necessary Angel: Essays on Reality and the Imagination.* New York: Vintage Books.

Strange, Adario, dir. 2004. *Hikikomori: Tokyo Plastic.* BAHX Films.

Strawson, Galen. 1986. *Freedom and Belief.* Oxford: Oxford University Press.

Tateno, Masaru, Tae Woo Park, Takahiro A. Kato, Wakako Umene-Nakano, and Toshikazu Saito. 2012. "Hikikomori as a Possible Clinical Term in Psychiatry: A Questionnaire Survey." *BMC Psychiatry* 12, no. 1: 169. DOI: 10.1186/1471-244X-12-169.

Teo, Alan R. 2012. "Social Isolation Associated with Depression: A Case Report of *Hikikomori*." *International Journal of Social Psychiatry* 59, no. 4: 339–41. DOI: 10.1177/0020764012437128.

Teo, Alan R., K.W. Stufflebaum, and T.A. Kato. 2014. "The Intersection of Culture and Solitude: The Hikikomori Phenomenon in Japan." In *The Handbook of Solitude: Psychological Perspectives on Social Isolation, Social Withdrawal, and Being Alone,* edited by Robert J. Coplan and Julie C. Bowker, 445–57. Oxford: Wiley-Blackwell.

Tillich, Paul. 1952. *The Courage to Be.* New Haven: Yale University Press.

Thrush, Laurence, dir. 2008. *Tobira no Muko* [*Beyond the Door*]. Size and Growth Films.

Todd, Kathleen Hunter Lea. 2011. "Hikikomania: Existential Horror or National Malaise?" *Southeast Review of Asian Studies* 33: 135–47.

Twenge, Jean. 2006. *Generation Me: Why Today's Young Americans are More Confident, Assertive, Entitled — and More Miserable than Ever Before.* New York: Free Press.

Twenge, Jean, and W. Keith Campbell. 2009. *The Narcissism Epidemic: Living in the Age of Entitlement.* New York: Simon and Schuster.

Uebel, Michael. 2013. "Psychoanalysis and the Question of Violence: From Masochism to Shame." *American Imago* 69, no. 4: 473–505. https://www.jstor.org/stable/26305034.

Umeda, Michael, and Norito Kawakami. 2012. "Association of Childhood Family Environments with the Risk of Social Withdrawal ('*Hikikomori*') in the Community Population in Japan." *Psychiatry and Clinical Neurosciences* 66, no. 2: 121–29. DOI: 0.1111/j.1440-1819.2011.02292.x.

Van Vugt, Mark, and Charlotte L. Hardy. 2010. "Cooperation for Reputation: Wasteful Contributions as Costly Signals in Public Goods." *Group Processes and Intergroup Relations* 13, no. 1: 101–11. DOI: 10.1177/1368430209342258.

Vermote, Rudi. 2017. "The Sane and the Insane Psychotic: 'Attacks on Linking' Revisited from Bion's Later Work."

In *Attacks on Linking Revisited: A New Look at Bion's Classic Work,* edited by Catalina Bronstein and Edna O'Shaughnessy, 76–86. London: Karnac.

Volkan, Vamik D. 1985. "'Suitable Targets of Externalization' and Schizophrenia." In *Toward a Comprehensive Model for Schizophrenic Disorders: Psychoanalytic Essays in Memory of Ping-Nie Pao, M.D.*, edited by David B. Feinsilver, 125–53. New York: Analytic Press.

Walton, Douglas N. 1986. *Courage: A Philosophical Investigation.* Berkeley: University of California Press.

Warshaw, Brette. 2019. "What's the Difference Between Courage and Bravery?" *What's the Difference?* March 5. https://www.whatsthediff.org/blog/2019/03/05/whats-the-difference-between-courage-and-bravery.

Watson, Gary. 1996. "Two Faces of Responsibility." *Philosophical Topics* 24, no. 2: 227–48. https://www.jstor.org/stable/43154245.

Watters, Ethan. 2010. *Crazy Like Us: The Globalization of the American Psyche.* New York: Free Press.

Watts, Jonathan. 2002. "Public Health Experts Concerned about 'Hikikomori.'" *The Lancet* 359, no. 9312: 1131. DOI: 10.1016/s0140-6736(02)08186-2.

Winnicott, D.W. 1953. "Transitional Objects and Transitional Phenomena: A Study of the First Not-me Possession." *International Journal of Psycho-Analysis* 34: 89–97.

———. 1965. *The Maturational Processes and the Facilitating Environment: Studies in the Theory of Emotional Development.* Edited by M. Khan. London: Hogarth and the Institute of Psycho-Analysis.

———. 1986. *Home Is Where We Start From: Essays by a Psychoanalyst.* Edited by C. Winnicott, R. Shepard, and M. Davis. New York: W.W. Norton.

———. 1989. *Psycho-analytic Explorations.* Edited by C. Winnicott, R. Shepherd, and M. Davis. Cambridge: Harvard University Press.

Ziarek, Ewa. 1993. "Kristeva and Levinas: Mourning, Ethics, and the Feminine." In *Ethics, Politics, and Difference in Julia*

Kristeva's Writing, edited by Kelly Oliver, 62–78. New York: Routledge. DOI: 10.4324/9780203760222-5.

Zielenziger, Michael. 2006. "Retreating Youth Become Japan's 'Lost Generation.' Interview with Michelle Norris." *National Public Radio,* November 25. http://www.npr.org/templates / story/story.php?storyId=6535284.